Just
Add
Jesus

Just Add Jesus

A Christian's Recipe for Leading a Life of Happiness and Satisfaction

James Stuart Bell and Gary Wilde

Adams Media
Avon, Massachusetts

Published by Adams Media, an F+W Publications Company
57 Littlefield Street
Avon, MA 02322
www.adamsmedia.com

ISBN: 1-59337-554-9
Printed in Canada.
J I H G F E D C B A

Library of Congress Cataloging-in-Publication Data
Bell, James Stuart.
Just add Jesus : a Christian's recipe for leading a life of
happiness andsatisfaction / James Stuart Bell and Gary Wilde
p.   cm.
ISBN 1-59337-554-9
1. Christian life. I. Wilde, Gary. II. Title.
BV4501.3.B452 2006
248.4--dc22
2005033316

This publication is designed to provide accurate and authoritative information with regard to the subject matter covered. It is sold with the understanding that the publisher is not engaged in rendering legal, accounting, or other
professional advice. If legal advice or other expert assistance is required, the
services of a competent professional person should be sought.

—From a *Declaration of Principles* jointly adopted by a Committee of the
American Bar Association anda Committee of Publishers and Associations

Many of the designations used by manufacturers and sellers to distinguish
their products are claimed as trademarks. Where those designations appear
in this book and Adams Media was aware of a trademark claim, the designations have been printed with initial capital letters.

This book is available at quantity discounts for bulk purchases.
For information, please call 1-800-872-5627.

To my mother, Joann Browning, who first brought me to Jesus.

—Gary Wilde

Contents

A Note to the Reader / ix

Introduction: A Great Addition for Your Life / xi

1. When you long to be settled . . . / 1

2. When you'd like to fib a little . . . / 8

3. When you need an encouraging friend . . . / 15

4. When you've failed to meet expectations . . . / 21

5. When you're feeling jealous . . . / 28

6. When your family really needs you . . . / 35

7. When you need a mentoring influence . . . / 43

8. When you'd like to remove your mask . . . / 50

9. When you seek a more genuine faith . . . / 59

10. When you're weary of rescuing (or being rescued) . . . / 65

11. When you need a peaceful spirit at home . . . / 72

12.   When you're dealing with a "problem person" . . . / 79

13.   When you wonder where to set your boundaries . . . / 85

14.   When you long for a sense of community . . . / 91

15.   When you need solid answers about religion . . . / 98

16.   When you face tough ethical choices . . . / 109

17.   When you want to trust others more . . . / 119

18.   When your Dad isn't there . . . / 123
19.   When you'd like to reach out with love's message . . . / 133

Appendix: This Awesome Jesus / 139

A Note to the Reader

We're so pleased to be able to make this book a joint effort, for, as Jesus said: "where two or three come together in my name, there am I with them."

Just Add Jesus is not only a product of individual introspection, but in a sense, it is a community effort, in which both authors invite the Spirit to move in their midst. Often this adds a desirable creative tension, for we experience Jesus in different ways, hear him speak uniquely and particularly to our one-of-a-kind existence. In this way, through our discussion and collaboration, we offer not only raw experience but, hopefully, a holy refinement of experience, as it is simmered in mutual reflection, discussion, and prayer.

And yet sometimes the "we" has its limitations and its awkwardness. "We" has the ring of the royal, the removed, the authoritative, unless we reserve it for those times when we mean *you,* too. Adding Jesus isn't about "we," it's about you and me and him. So past the point of this page, we will tell our stories and our thoughts in the singular first person, the "I." In the introduction, that "I" is Jim, who wrote it. In the chapters that follow, that "I" is Gary, starting with stories told from his personal point of view. We hope this "I" makes this book that much more accessible and immediate, that it will help *you* realize that *we* come to you in all humility and fellowship.

Introduction

A Great Addition for Your Life

Think of the blending of two substances: "just add cream" to coffee, for instance. Where does the black coffee end and the cream begin? Adding Jesus' self to our self creates a similar blending. One biblical saint who did this concluded, "It is no longer I who live but [he] who lives in me, yet nonetheless I live." Where does the life of one, and the life of the other, begin and end?

The *blended* place is a *blessed* place. And this movement of "adding" applies to any good thing we desire within the will of God. It could be overcoming negative habits or learning how to be a better wife or husband. It could be enjoying alone time or reaching out to a neighbor in distress. But certainly it goes beyond asking, "What would Jesus do?" to enquire, How would Jesus *be* . . . here . . . now . . . *with* me in this? That's the essence of adding Jesus.

Can anyone do it? Yes. But it requires an openness to love, a letting go into being loved, graced, freely accepted. We all constantly scan the horizon for more—the warmth of a helping hand; a friend who comes alongside and picks us up, dusts us off, and says, "Let us walk along now together. You may fall again . . . and again and again . . . but I'll be there with you."

The Buddha was certainly right in saying we reap what we sow. But I see Jesus constantly going beyond pure justice, thrusting us into mercy. His is the message of a gracious uplifting, a reliance on a loving *person* rather than a karmic force. When you add Jesus, you add heavenly warmth. In his short time on earth, Jesus didn't go around handing out Bibles. Nor did he write inspiring manuscripts or build beautiful houses of worship. Instead, he made disciples; that is, he gave to the world . . . *persons.*

Therefore, if his work on earth is to be done at all, it will be carried out, in large part, by warm flesh and blood—we who are opening our hearts to him, adding him to our thinking, to our decisions, to our words and actions. We will help those who fall (as we ourselves have been helped to our feet), we will spread the message of his love, and we will lean on him for the strength to keep going.

If relying on a person is considered using a crutch, so be it. No doubt we were never meant to stand and walk on our own.

He's with Us, but *How*?

I wish I could have been there on the thunder-and-lightning-ringed mountain when Moses received the Ten Commandments from the hand of God. To actually see, to really *know,* This is God at work, without a doubt. What could be better?

Rarely do we get a blazing object lesson from the gates of glory, though. Rather, we must learn how to see Jesus in the tiny dots of light scattered into our days.

So often his guidance emerges in our inner thoughts as the still, small voice within us. It is a sound that can't quite be explained with our rational minds. Yet, it is a sense of rightness when we have made a decision, a quality of conviction when we have sought the truth, a recognition that something feels like it fits, though we can't prove it.

This gentle undertone may carry emotions with it, but ultimately it supersedes emotion. For me, it is an internal suggestion, a veiled hint that comes through people, events, books, or art. And the message is affirmed in various ways, often in moments of solitude. The consequence is that silence and listening will be key components in adding Jesus.

When you spend time in silence, you may find yourself contemplating questions like these:

What does it mean for me that Jesus promises to stay close?

How might I expect to encounter him as I walk through my day and move around in my relationships?

Am I to look for bright and shining revelations from the mountaintop?

Actually, the Bible tells us he will mostly speak in a gentle whisper. What is the key to hearing this divine murmur? You might try just being with Jesus for a quarter of an hour, simply waiting in silence, or you could experiment with prayer a bit. (Most people do pray, whether they call it that or not—the heart speaks, even when we can find no words for our lips.) Any of us can learn this kind of listening, calmly attending to our circumstances for the words of wisdom they whisper. Then we'll begin to name the things that seem to be saying yes and no to us. And we'll remain open to the possibility that within them is Jesus' quiet voice. This is adding Jesus.

And that voice is not just for the times of trouble, or for when we're hurting—though it is good to turn to him then. He is a helper, yes, but he is also a master. I think of the clergyman who was visiting a very sick woman in the hospital. The woman greeted the minister by saying, "I'm glad you're here, but I don't want to be clichéd to death. Just talk about anything else, but not religion, please."

I can respect a person like that. She'd had her fill of the kind of religion that had no edge, that was soft and "nice." She thought of religion as mere cliché—shopworn phrases, routinely applied to everyone, insensitive to her individual needs. However, Jesus' voice may have an edge to it, as he, the master, invites his followers to do better.

Satisfying . . . and Dangerous?

Jesus will extend that invitation to you, and sugarcoated clichés will not be enough. And that Jesus is a stumbling block to so many folks these days—until they realize he comes with love but not with sweet sentimentality or the vapid grin of a kind-but-senile granddaddy who makes no demands whatsoever. Then they become more interested, even enthused. Because who could want a sovereign lord who never requires a thing? Knowing a loving Lord, who also challenges us to grow and thrive, is a great blessing.

In one of C. S. Lewis's fiction books, *The Lion, the Witch and the Wardrobe,* Aslan the lion represents the person of Jesus. A character named Lucy contemplates what it will be like to meet him, asking, "Is he—quite safe?"

The answer comes: "Safe? . . . Who said anything about safe? 'Course he isn't safe. But he's good. He's the King, I tell you."

We hold here that Jesus is not "safe." Consider a dangerous question: *What is it about my life that I'd like to face squarely today?* Isn't it always better to stay in direct contact with hard truth than to slide through life clinging to sentimental self-deception? The story of Jesus is weighty this way, not totally safe. His message is warm and gracious but in no way trivial; his love gentle but never offered with a ticket to easy living. We do well to be in awe of him and to approach him in expectant hope with a healthy dose of reverence.

Perhaps that's the best way to read the coming chapters: in reverent hopefulness. This book came together as the "Jesus-adding concept" grew and developed in my mind. I also knew that I needed to ground the spiritual truths flowing from it with the concrete experiences of ordinary life, told through

Gary's stories. Much of this book centers around stories told by my coauthor, Gary, gathered from his own life and those of dear friends.

You won't find that these occurrences are earth-shattering or unusual. Rather, they seem to be so down-to-earth accessible. I think every reader who approaches them with an open heart will be moved to say, "Yes, he indeed tells of *me!*"

In this book, I will invite you to immerse yourself in our joint interpretation of how you can "add Jesus," and Gary's willingness to share his heart in remarkable transparency. Each chapter will begin with an experience to share, hoping to pull you in by naming something that is, in its *concrete* detail, something that is, ultimately, a *universal* problem, feeling, or longing. When we are together in that place, we human beings invite Jesus there—his words, his actions, or simply his person. So we have two places: where *we* are and where Jesus is. And the two places need to come together somehow, to synthesize in a new reality, the realness of a new spiritual life for us to live. That fascinating synthesis happens as we keep asking: *How would it be for me to add Jesus to my world at just this point of my experience—to my genuine need, struggle, conflict, dream, aspiration, joy?*

That's really all there is to it. Then it's simply a matter of letting Jesus have his "space" in our lives. And here is a delicious paradox, because one of Jesus' names of old is *Immanuel,* meaning "God with us." If we can learn to really be where we are, fully aware of the truth of our lives—no fudging or excuses—we will find Jesus already there with us. Maybe that's why the world's religions constantly stress a most foundational task in growing the spiritual life: "Know thyself."

Amazingly, that is what it means to be called by him to take a step closer. Within the conflict between these two "places"— what I know of me and what I know of my Creator—a synthesis blossoms forth. The "adding" is simply a turn of mind, a *metanoia,* which is the Bible's word for repentance.

All of this is why we're really not trying to offer a solution or an answer in all the simple stories you'll read. For ultimately, when Jesus enters, he enters not as a formula, a strategy, or a plan. He enters as a person. He asks us to "be" with him, where he is, always: closer than our next breath. And that is far more than enough to satisfy.

In each chapter that follows here, we invite you into the conversation, this dialectic, constantly asking the question along with you: If I were to look to him in this situation, if I invited Jesus here—right now—how would the situation be transformed? More to the point, how would *I* be transformed?

Yes, you will be changed. No one comes into close contact with this fascinating person without a thorough makeover. Are you ready?

> *If anyone be in Christ, he is a new creature.*
> *Old things are passed away;*
> *behold, all things are new.*
> —James Stuart Bell

1. When you long to be settled . . .

Just Add Jesus

I lived in Chicago, right downtown, and life was often hectic, fast paced, and draining. So it made sense that this kind of question would surface in my mind as I drove back from a trip in the country: *Is it possible in this life just to be content—just to* live, *without all the striving and struggling?*

I was headed back to the Windy City, driving through miles and miles of cornfields in southern Illinois, passing through the tiniest of small towns, one by one, separated by long stretches of flat, state-road pavement. Everything about those little towns looked so blissfully settled, peaceful, and serene. Each quaint community, with its couple of white-steepled churches, its inevitable grain elevator, its rows of clapboard houses with impeccably manicured lawns and flower beds, spoke to me of a

heavenly existence, far from the cacophony of the subway tracks and blaring sirens that would soon envelope me once again. Surely these were places where a man and his family could live out their days in peace and warmth and love.

Boy, imagine living in a place like this: Get up in the morning, go to work—in the fields or at the feed store—come home, play with the kids, sit in the lawn chair, watch the sun go down, and go to bed in peace. We're talking hassle-free living here, far from the rat race. Wow!

But, of course, it was all a fantasy—pleasant and compelling—but a fantasy nonetheless. For I knew that each picket-fenced yard harbored a house where real people lived, with all of their unique problems and struggles. If I could exchange my hectic pace for their seemingly tranquil way of life, perhaps I would. But I know I'd just be inheriting a brand-new set of problems, too. There's no escape from that.

Yet what can I do when I really need a sense of settledness and contentment in life?

Where Did Jesus Live?

Many people secretly believe they can create the perfect situation or environment for themselves and their families. They are thus constantly harried with the "fix-ups" that this requires them to perform—on machines or houses or even on the personalities in their families. In effect, they are trying to make their life on earth perfect—a veritable heaven-on-earth reality.

I myself am a constant practitioner of this art of life perfecting. But I haven't yet been too successful. And then I see Jesus living the wanderer's life. From all we see of him in the Bible, he's living a life of purposeful chaos. Moving from one town to the next, preaching, teaching, healing, but always seeming to let others set his agenda. If we were making a documentary of his typical week, it would be a travelogue, and we'd have to keep moving. Because there he is again, walking, sailing, hiking up the mountain—following the flow of physical needs, of burning questions, of constant challenges. . . .

"Lord, my daughter is dying. Please come quick!"
"Rabbi, I heard you could cast out demons. Help!"
"Look over here! We caught her in adultery!"
"Can you get us something to eat, Master?"
"But my son is so sick. Hurry!"
"We're afraid of this storm—and you're sleeping?"
"Hey, who do you think you are, preaching like that?"
"Hey, who do you think you . . . are?"

And where does he stay? Where does he actually live?

Mainly, with friends. And when the friends leave him, he camps out. We know this is true, because Jesus himself tells us. A man once walked up to him and said, "I will follow you wherever you go." But apparently this prospective disciple didn't realize how little security such a commitment might bring to his life. "Foxes have holes and birds of the air have nests," Jesus told him. "But the Son of Man has no place to lay his head" (Luke 9:58). How is that for a bit of unsettledness about the future?

So Jesus continues walking forward into his daily chaos of pressing needs and *savoring each poignant moment.*

As always, he comes through to me as a man of paradoxical complexity. He constantly makes me realize that the opposite of a truth is not always an *un*truth. That sometimes it can be a deeper, profounder truth still. Therefore, the one who had no place to lay his head could also make an astonishing promise to any who add him to their lives. He said . . .

> ✑ Do not let your hearts be troubled.
> Trust in God; trust also in me.
> In my Father's house are many rooms;
> if it were not so, I would have told you.
> I am going there to prepare
> a place for you.
>
> And if I go and prepare a place for you,
> I will come back
> and take you to be with me
> that you also may be where I am.
>
> —John 14:1–3

Jesus is telling his followers that he is leaving this earth but preparing a permanent home in heaven for them. They are going to miss his physical presence on earth but they need not be anxious. Not only are they guaranteed to be with him forever in eternity when they die, but he is going to give them his Spirit to live in them while they are still here.

So when I get anxious or discontented, I can be assured that if I've added Jesus to my life, he lives inside me. He is the shelter I can run to and find peace, safety, and provision in. It also makes me think, if I bring Jesus into my life at the point of my need for security, will he ask me to live—at least for the time being—with even a little less comfort and certainty about the temporary things around me? I like the way the hero of the 1993 film *Shadowlands* (a fictionalized biography of the writer C. S. Lewis) put it: "The settled happiness and security which we all desire, God withholds from us by the very nature of the world: but joy, pleasure, and merriment he has scattered abroad. We are never safe, but we have plenty of fun, and some ecstasy. . . . Our Father refreshes us on the journey with some pleasant inns, but will not encourage us to mistake them for home."

While I'm Here

So, even this moment, as I face another excruciatingly busy day, I keep wondering, *is it wrong to seek contentment?*

Are you asking it too? And how do you, personally, handle the longings and frustrations of feeling not-yet-arrived?

I've come to a cautious conclusion: Maybe it's okay to embrace that longing, to invite it in and live with it as a normal part of my humanness . . . *if.* If I learn to give thanks that, when any moment of heart-deep satisfaction comes, it is always temporary, a fleeting preview to a better existence.

Today I am going to let myself experience some bliss, if it should enter my hours, or even some ecstasy, if it should grace one or two precious moments. But I won't demand a settled contentment, and I promise not to mistake these refreshing resting places for heaven, my true destination. No, at least not today; for each day comes and goes, but I can look forward to an eternity with Jesus, who has a special and permanent place reserved just for me.

For this is not yet home, no matter how hard I try to make it so. I'm quite sure there will always be a steep relational mountain to climb, a gut-wrenching trial to face, a scary risk to take. It's called living by faith, whether I live in Chicago . . . or even if I move someday to a little house with a wooden porch that overlooks Route 55 and a few square miles of corn.

Adding to the Mix

"[This] life is the preparation, the training ground, the place where God begins his work of making us into what he wants us to be. But it is not our home."

Your God Is Too Small, *by J. B. Phillips*

For the Week Ahead with Jesus

During a moment of quiet this week, consider directing your attention to this statement: "If you have to move even ten inches from where you are now in order to be happy, you never will be."

Then chart your family's *past* moves (with dates, places, reasons for the move, and level of resulting happiness) over the years. Ask yourself:

    ❧   Were any of our moves undertaken because of boredom, restlessness, envy, status seeking, or other unhappy motives?

    ❧   If Jesus were a part of my thinking about the true meaning of "home," what would it mean for our next move?

2. When you'd like to fib a little . . .

Just Add Jesus

The thing about adding Jesus is that it's not just a mental exercise or a nice philosophical abstraction. When Jesus enters, our lives change. They just have to transform. Let me offer a couple of examples. Two friends of mine—coincidentally, both named John—were tempted to lie. One was a young minister at the time; the other was a college student. Here are the stories they told me.

John 1's Story

For two hours, the questions had flowed incessantly. Not that the setting was uncomfortable. Quite the contrary. The mood had remained warmly engaging during this most important day of my foreseeable future. There at an island summer home, under the benevolent eye of bald eagles and goldfinches as well as the intense

scrutiny of a pastoral nominating committee, I was inter-
viewing for my dream position.

They're making this easy, I thought as I spieled off answers
to questions I knew as well as my name. I was doing great.
People's body language was saying, This could amount to
something.

Next question: "John, could you tell us about your personal spiritual practices?" *Yikes! Now what do I say?* I smiled.
"Good question, especially for a minister." *Weak, John. They
can tell you're buying time. But what do I say? I don't have a
devotional life! Well, not a very impressive one.*

*Hmmm. I could make one up: An hour a day of prayer and
meditation; never miss. God so blesses the time that I'd be at a
loss if ever I skipped—*

No. Forget it.

"How's my spiritual life? Miserable. I wish I could tell you
different, but it's sadly true: I'm not very good at it. It's a great
mystery to me how I can know how valuable a quiet time is
and yet be so incompetent at having one. In fact, if I were to
come as your associate pastor, I could use your help with this."

*There, I'd done it. Bye, bye job. Who'd want a minister with
more excuses than spiritual devotion?*

In God's grand scheme of things, somebody obviously
considered openness at least as important as piety. A couple
of weeks later, the committee voted unanimously to call me.
I'm sure my pathetic devotional practices didn't further my
cause, but neither did they derail it.

Today, several months after the move, I'm sitting staring at a "Residential Real Property Disclosure Report" requiring an honest accounting of my previous home's defects. For six months this unsold, empty house, parasitically devouring both my earnings and our savings, has been the unforeseen bane of our move.

Now—finally—we have a prospective buyer. And now—dreadfully—I've got to answer such questions as, "I am aware of material defects in the basement or foundation." Well, there is that one little foundation crack I noticed by the garage door, but who's to know if I've seen it or not? And why would I want to set inspectors onto the trail of anything that might blow this deal?

"Yes" or "No" are my only choices.

John 2's Story

Old Faithful—dependable and predictable, just like clockwork. That's pretty much me. Can't stand disorder (except for the clutter in my junk room). In any kind of group or committee, I'm usually the self-appointed person who plans ahead to remind everybody of the meeting, who makes sure we have a discussion leader, who settles what chapter of the book we're reading next week.

Also, I'm generally stable in other areas, like morals, too (except for secret sins). However, I've "bailed out" on my dependable ethical standards a very few times. One time was in college. They had a skip-as-many-classes-as-you-want rule if you upheld a certain grade average. I have a bad back, and I hated attending one afternoon class that was dull, dull, dull. Sitting in those stiff, wooden desks was torture, so my high grade average was deliverance.

Then one day, the physical education teacher didn't show for his class—at least not on time. He had sent one guy out with a bow and arrow for that day's session. We all rebelled at learning the fine art of archery . . . and played football, instead.

Enter phys ed teacher looking enraged. He took the roll. "Did you play football?" was the question to each of us, in turn. I knew if he gave me an F, my grade-point average was shot, and it was back to Dull Class 201. I lied.

I had the reputation of being a "Jesus freak" on campus. Yet in a tough situation, I bailed out.

Oh, That Pressurized Feeling!

Can you feel the pressure in these two guys to do the right thing? The guilt at failing? That's what it means to say that when Jesus enters our lives, we feel compelled to change our ways. Only the influence of his presence tells us to bother.

Yet when the pressure cooker gets turned up on a "Jesus-added person," even she will tend to bail out in certain predictable ways. There's the workaholic or sportsaholic or foodaholic. For some, pornography or rage becomes an escape hatch, a way they "hit the road" spiritually. For others, it's going on shopping sprees or just becoming obsessed with a clean house. The simple question that needs to arise in this chapter is, What escape do you turn to when life's submarine feels too pressurized? When you're tempted to let go of your ethical integrity? In the New Testament, the standard word for patience, or perseverance, literally means "remaining under."

It's tough, isn't it, to remain under the pressure, stable and dependable, looking to the Lord for help to stay the course with integrity?

Who knew this better than the disciple called Peter, a man well known for a particularly famous, fibbing fakery:

> ✑ Now Peter was sitting out in the courtyard, and a servant girl came to him. "You also were with Jesus of Galilee," she said. But he denied it before them all. "I don't know what you're talking about," he said.
>
> Then he went out to the gateway, where another girl saw him and said to the people there, "This fellow was with Jesus of Nazareth." He denied it again, with an oath: "I don't know the man!"
>
> After a little while, those standing there went up to Peter and said, "Surely you are one of them, for your accent gives you away."
>
> Then he began to call down curses on himself and he swore to them, "I don't know the man!" Immediately a rooster crowed. Then Peter remembered the word Jesus had spoken: "Before the rooster crows, you will disown me three times." And he went outside and wept bitterly.
>
> —Matthew 26:69–75

The beautiful thing about this story is that it is not the *end* of the story. In fact, as Peter walked with Jesus, learning from him and growing spiritually strong, he eventually received some wonderful affirmations and promotions, as shown in Matthew 16:18–19. He was . . .

Heralded as the rock of the church;
Given the keys to the kingdom;
Told to feed the church that Jesus left to him.

In a stroke of precious and gentle irony, just before Jesus left the earth for heaven, he asked Peter, "Do you love me?" three times; Peter had the chance to atone for his previous denials. Three times, Peter proclaimed his love.

And, as always, before long, the way of Jesus became the way of self-sacrifice. Peter taught and worked hard for the kingdom and was eventually crucified for his faith—upside down. (You see, he felt unworthy to die the same kind of death as his master. He had long been cured of fakery.)

Adding to the Mix

Jesus is the only completely free person I have ever encountered. . . . A really free person is able to laugh when others are bitter; he can be kind when others hate; he can be in a room full of gossip and not participate; he can be himself no matter what pressures are on him. Jesus was free.

—Unhappy Secrets of the Christian Life,
by Philip Yancey and Tim Stafford

Dare to be true: nothing can need a lie;
A fault which needs it most, grows two thereby.
—The Church Porch, by George Herbert

For the Week Ahead with Jesus

During a time of quiet this week, think back through the previous three months and consider some of the pressure points that have plagued you. Ask yourself:

- How well have I handled the pressure?

- In what ways was I tempted to bail out—fib or fake it?

- What would I do differently, if I could have a second chance?

- If Jesus were sitting in the chair across from me, what might he say about all of this?

Now find a Bible and read through Philippians 3:7–4:1. What do you think this passage is saying to you? If you feel moved to do so, offer thanks to God, in your own way, for his strength to persevere during the tempting times.

3. When you need an encouraging friend . . .

Just Add Jesus

I made a foolish move . . . and plummeted headlong into one of the lowest valleys of my life. Some responsibilities were suddenly shifted at work, a colleague was placed over me, I got angry and resigned.

Actually, I thought I had another job in hand—I was absolutely certain it would come to pass. I was going to work with a good friend of mine someplace else. He had already formally interviewed me twice, and I was to be hired after he returned from overseas within three months. So I walked off my job, convinced that as soon as Charles returned, I would start my new position. Thus began a nerve-wracking three months of depleting our family savings and my pension pay-out. But I was looking ahead with hope.

Then Charles returned and told me that I had just one more small hoop to jump through in

order to complete the interview process: a little ten-minute meeting with his boss, a mere formality. I entered the boss's office a happy man. Five minutes later, I was completely devastated. Charles's boss rejected me out of hand: "No way you are going to work here."

Both Charles and I were stunned. I went home, sat on the living room floor, and broke down in tears: *Why me, God? My money is gone, my wife and two little boys have needs, we've just bought our first new house. What's going on here?* I saw visions of my family on the streets in short order. It's probably the lowest, the most scared, I've ever been.

A Silent Heaven

But God wasn't answering—at least, not in a way I could hear at the time. So, what do you do when you need comfort, encouragement—help—and even heaven itself seems silent?

It's not that I wanted someone to come along and solve all my problems. I knew I'd made some poor decisions, and I was willing to work hard to try to solve them. No, I simply wanted to know that I wasn't left alone, and be able to *feel* it so.

I thought of the old story about the little girl who'd been put to bed one night and was just dozing off when a tremendous flash of lightning, accompanied by the roar of thunder, woke her with a jolt. She cried out, and her father came to comfort her. She said, "Daddy, the storm is so bad, and I'm scared!" Her father assured her that, although she couldn't see it, love was all around her and would protect her. The child listened carefully to what her father said. But then there was another terrible flash of lightning and loud thunder. The little girl said, "Oh, Daddy, please stay here with me. I know that love is all around me. But just for tonight, I need some love *with skin on it!*"

That was it, exactly. I needed someone, here, now, to hold my life and carry my burdens in the midst of a storm—just for a while, until I could get my equilibrium back.

Have you been there too? And the last time you asked, "Why me, God?" . . . what kind of answer did you receive?

If there was silence, perhaps it's because God has already provided a way for us in all such situations. I'm talking about a rule, or law, for us to live by, and it comes from Jesus. In the Bible, it's referred to like this: "Carry each other's burdens, and in this way, you will fulfill the law of Christ" (Galatians 6:2). If you would like to hear it directly from Jesus' mouth, here it is: "A new command I give you: Love one another. As I have loved you, so you must love one another. By this all men will know that you are my disciples, if you love one another" (John 13:34–35).

When I need a lighter load . . . the Lord sends someone to lift?
When I long for a kind word . . . he sends a speaker?
When I ask for comfort . . . he sends a friend?

When I need Jesus, he may send his servant? Yes! Jesus often enters with the hands and feet of a loving neighbor, an encouraging friend. Think about it: Who, for you, has been that kind of "saint," someone who reached out to you during a time of trial? What things did this person do to help? At those times, *to add Jesus to your hurting days is to receive comfort from his people.* Again, the Bible has a nice way of summing it all up:

Praise be to the God and Father of our Lord Jesus Christ, the Father of compassion and the God of all comfort, who comforts us in all our troubles, so that we can comfort those in any trouble with the comfort we ourselves have received from God.

—*2 Corinthians 1:3–4*

A Helping Hand

What got me through that horrendous year of job loss and job searching? I wish I could say it was my unwavering faith in my Lord Jesus. In fact, during that whole time, he seemed mostly absent, at least painfully silent. And it is truly difficult to maintain a stiff upper lip through times like those. Hard to maintain a firm faith. Yet, it surely was Jesus' gracious, undergirding arm supporting me through the encouraging words and actions of my friend Charles.

This brother-in-Jesus stuck with me through it all, calling me, constantly passing along tips and leads about work I could get. I felt I had to be carried, one step at a time, by a brother who chose to take up the burden on my behalf, ushering me through a dark tunnel of despair into the light of a brand-new career.

And here's the most wonderful—and challenging—aspect of the whole story: it behooves all of us to be ready both to receive and to give the comfort that God supplies to his creatures. So, if I've been through a crushing trial and I come out alive, I can now turn my eyes to focus on those around me. Who is suffering in silence at the office, for example? Who is living daily in silent pain, keeping the pasted-on smile firmly in place? Who needs a comforting shoulder and a listening ear? Can I "be Jesus" for him or her right now?

Adding to the Mix

God raises up among us some true saints to help us along the way. These are not perfect people, but they have received an unusual abundance of grace that radiates the larger divine wisdom and love in such a way that our own souls are illuminated. . . . [Let us] listen deeply to them when they appear, so that we can recognize our own soul's deep callings in their mirror.

—*Tilden Edwards, director, Shalem Institute*

What does love look like? It has the hands to help others. It has the feet to hasten to the poor and needy. It has eyes to see misery and want. It has the ears to hear the sighs and sorrows of men. That is what love looks like.

—*St. Augustine*

For the Week Ahead with Jesus

During a quiet time this week, use a sheet of paper or a page in your journal to sketch a "tribulation history" of your adult life. This will be an up-and-down line graph showing the major trials, crises, and setbacks that you have endured so far. Include dates, if possible.

With arrows pointing to particular periods of your life, jot forms of encouragement that you recall receiving during those times and who gave them to you. Then recall the ways in which you have experienced comfort from Jesus. Try to remember how that comfort came to you, and jot down the events and persons associated with that comfort.

Use your tribulation-history graph as the basis for a few moments of prayer. Offer thanks for the people who have been encouragers. Offer praise for the blessings and comfort from Jesus that you have experienced during and after tough times. Finally, offer any requests for further help or for the healing of wounds that remain from those trials.

*E*ncountering success at every turn sounds like a prescription for perfect happiness, right? Very early in his life, Jean knew what he wanted to be. He had significant musical abilities, and his parents provided every opportunity for him to develop them. With parents who were professional musicians themselves, he had many advantages helping him develop quickly into a fine violinist. The problem, however, was this: he was developing a view of life that suggested things would always fall into place for him. He had no idea he was falling for this subtle distortion of reality. And so life continued on its seemingly predictable path. His parents were thrilled at his success, and he was thrilled at their approval.

Then came the day when things didn't turn out like Jean, or they, wanted. It was the violin competition in his hometown, where he was returning

after two years of music conservatory schooling. He had, surprisingly, garnered only third place in this same competition when he was in high school. This time around, given the additional training he'd undertaken, he expected to win.

So he played his heart out, swaying with the intricate rhythms of a Bach two-part invention. His bowing was precise, his tuning right on pitch, and his passion flowed into the instrument, washing out over a seemingly rapt audience.

Yet, when the results were announced, he wasn't mentioned among the winners. "My mother was seated next to me," Jean told me, recalling that day years ago. "I can still remember her comment: 'The judging wasn't *fair!*' She yelled it loud enough to be heard by other competitors and their families. Everybody looked up with shock in their eyes. I was disappointed not to be a prizewinner but also embarrassed at my mother's outburst. I've had other successes and other less-than-successful experiences since that day—but none of them with my mother at my side in the same way. I felt I really let her down."

It's Still about the Folks

They say that no matter how old we are, we still want our parents' approval. Have you noticed that desire in yourself? Even if your parents are long gone from this earth—or even if you hardly ever knew them at all—isn't it true that you still harbor a deep and abiding yearning to hear their words of approval?

It's curious, then, that when Jesus lands in a situation perfectly suited for the bubbling forth of this innate longing, we see him—even as a twelve-year-old boy—looking to *another* source for approval, one more enduring than the fleeting impulses of human parents.

We might suppose most parents today would start looking through the stores in the mall, perhaps heading to the video-game area or the movie theater. But with Jesus, it would have to be the temple. He was a very religious young lad . . .

> ✍ They found him in the temple courts, sitting among the teachers, listening to them and asking them questions. Everyone who heard him was amazed at his understanding and his answers.
>
> When his parents saw him, they were astonished. His mother said to him, "Son, why have you treated us like this? Your father and I have been anxiously searching for you."
>
> —Luke 2:46–48

Here in Luke 2, we have the only glimpse of Jesus' adolescence the Bible allows us. Since the Scriptures are silent about Jesus and his development between infancy and manhood, no doubt this scene with his parents in the temple is quite important. Yet, if it is truly crucial, how can it be that the one event conveyed from Jesus' early childhood is the moment of *his failure to meet parental expectations?*

What does this say to you and me? At the very least, it must mean that pleasing our parents, or any human being, really can't be the ultimate goal of our lives. Jesus himself shows us this with his response, which comes forth as a gentle rebuke: "Why were you searching for me? . . . Didn't you know I had to be in my Father's house?" In effect, Jesus says there are things more important than approval on this earth—what we call success. There is such a thing as the approval of heaven. That is the important thing to seek. And it may sometimes look like failure, at least for a while. That's why, if we ask, "Was Jesus successful?" it's not immediately apparent how to answer . . .

He didn't write any best sellers.
He never won a military victory.
He couldn't be voted into political office.
He produced no great works of art.
He created no history-changing inventions.

Yet Jesus was the most successful human being who ever graced this earth. He lived with complete integrity. He always expressed the appropriate emotion. He never did or said anything that he could possibly regret. In short, he never sinned. He was perfect.

How's that for successful living? Furthermore, he fully accomplished the cosmos-altering mission that his heavenly Father had set for him: to save the world from sin. In doing so—which also involved an aspect of judgment—he thoroughly disappointed countless critics.

He still fails to meet their expectations.

He's just not *nice* enough.

And What's Your Failure Quotient?

Whose expectations are you meeting—or not—these days? And how much does it matter to you? In the midst of seeking approval, a natural human tendency, to add Jesus means adding a quality to your life that pushes against popular opinion, mitigates against conformity, and often compels confrontation with the forces of tradition. Are you ready for all of that?

Which brings us back to Jean, our violin-playing friend. In hindsight, Jean thinks that day of the music competition was absolutely crucial to his growth. Why? Because he had to start coming to terms, as a grown-up, with failure and disappointment. He also had to sift out his priorities and his responses to the bumps and bruises of life. "My mother envisioned nothing but a smooth road to the top for me," says Jean. "Yet I was no longer able to view my experience as a smooth ascent. In fact, maybe there were lessons along the way, in the dark places, that were part of what I needed to learn."

While Jean could have wished for a response from his mother that showed only concern for him ("I'm sorry that things didn't turn out better for you"), perhaps that day was blessed for him nonetheless. From that point on, he started developing his own perspective on success.

For any of us, that kind of growth, in itself, is a wonderfully effective foil to failure.

Adding to the Mix

To become a man, a son must first become a prodigal, leave home, and travel solo into a far country. Alien nation before reconciliation. There can be no homecoming without leave-taking.

—Sam Keen, philosopher

At the end of your life, you will never regret not having passed one more test, not winning one more verdict or not closing one more deal. You will regret time not spent with a husband, a friend, a child or a parent.

—Barbara Bush, former First Lady

For the Week Ahead with Jesus

Consider writing a letter to your mother or father this week, whether still living or not—a letter that you won't send. Write the letter in your journal or on a sheet of paper and include these topics:

- Joys and affirmations: Memories of the "good times," thankfulness for your guidance and care;

- Regrets: Things I wish I'd done or said in the past, things I wish you had done or said;

- Forgiveness areas: Ways I need forgiveness from you, ways I need to forgive you.

Option: Try writing the letter with your opposite hand. This can make you more vulnerable and help you connect with your feelings and your childlikeness. When you've finished the letter, think: In what ways am I still influenced by unresolved issues with my parent(s)? If Jesus were calling me into my next practical step toward freedom, what would I likely need to do?

Then throw the letter away, or keep it in a safe and private place.

I've spent almost five years in this place . . . and what do I really have to show for it? I was sitting across from my brother Jeff in the cramped church office of my first full-time pastorate, just before the Sunday worship service. A heavy mantle of discouragement pressed down on my shoulders. The little church was always a hotbox on bright summer mornings, and sweat was already popping out under my shirt collar. I could almost hear the paint chipping off the cracked plaster walls of the century-old frame building.

Of course, the warm fellowship at the church had been satisfying, but my salary was still so low that my wife and I struggled each month to pay our bills. And the ancient parsonage, though quaint and full of history, often felt as though it was sagging around our ears. Numerous members of the congregation were pulling down substantial

six-figure incomes and had beautiful homes but would still occasionally give us advice about "how you might budget a little better." I glanced down at the dead flies clustered on the dingy windowsill next to my garage-sale-special gray metal desk and felt a throb of green bile leap into my throat. Jealousy.

Jeff had been making out well in the inflationary real estate market of the seventies, a market I had passed up in favor of moving a thousand miles from home and dedicating my first decade of married life to the church. Three years younger than me, he had already bought and sold a couple of homes and profited nicely. I'd never owned my own home. *I'm way behind in this little game,* I thought, *and I'll never catch up. . . .*

About That *Other* Brother

In the words of the poet William Walsh, "I can endure my own despair, but not another's hope." That's quite common, isn't it? It seems easier to handle life's difficulties than to handle the good news in the life of a neighbor, or even in the life of a brother. If you're skeptical, then take a quick flight of imagination. Suppose your sibling or your best friend just won a lottery worth millions. Quick—how do you feel? If you have nothing but joy in your heart, then you can skip this chapter; you have arrived at a level of equanimity surpassing that of most readers of this book (and its authors).

But suppose we add Jesus to the mix. He had plenty of insight into our struggles with jealousy, and he raised the topic frequently. In one quite famous parable, he lays it on the line. We know it as the story of the prodigal (that is, rebellious) son. But we'll have to look at the *other* son, the rebel's older brother, to get the point about jealousy. You see, we know about the rebel son, the one who ran away and squandered his inheritance. But sometimes we gloss over the good older son, the one who was stuck with a seemingly terminal case of the greens. Let's review for a moment.

Son number two becomes restless, goes to Dad, and says, in violation of custom, that he wants his inheritance while his father is still alive. So Dad is generous, gives his younger son the money that was being kept for him, and wishes him well.

Off goes the young man to the big city, and he is not particularly intent on finding a good savings and loan for his funds. No, he's much more interested in the gambling tables, the ladies, and the parties accompanying both.

Result: instant poverty. Time to go home.

Meanwhile, the good son is working in the field as usual, when he hears music and dancing coming from the house. The servants are hollering, "Your little brother came home, and your dad has put on a big party for him. The kid is back and doing all right!"

✑ The older brother became angry and refused to go in. So his father went out and pleaded with him. But he answered his father, "Look! All these years I've been slaving for you and never disobeyed your orders. Yet you never gave me even a young goat so I could celebrate with my friends. But when this son of yours who has squandered your property with prostitutes comes home, you kill the fattened calf for him!"

—Luke 15:28–30

Don't be too hard on big brother. Try walking in his shoes for a moment. What would you be thinking?

Where's *My* Party?

Jealousy. Envy. It hurts; it feels like a lump of molten lead burning your insides. Why won't it go away?

   🖋 O, beware, my lord, of jealousy;
It is the green-eyed monster which doth mock
The meat it feeds on.
—William Shakespeare, from *Othello Act 3,* Scene 3

Shakespeare saw its true colors. And I'm sure you've been there with me in the company of this self-devouring monster. Everybody else has been invited to life's party, but we're left at home, alone, doing the dishes. It can overpower any of us. We look around and wonder, When do I get *my* share of the goodies? As feminist writer Erica Jong once defined it, "Jealousy is all the fun you think they had."

But it couldn't happen between a brother and sister, right? Wrong. Even among the disciples of Jesus, those dedicated followers who gave up everything to follow their master, we see the ugly green-eyed monster rearing its head:

> ✑ Then the mother of Zebedee's sons came to Jesus with her sons and, kneeling down, asked a favor of him.
> "What is it you want?" he asked.
> She said, "Grant that one of these two sons of mine may sit at your right and the other at your left in your kingdom."
> —Matthew 20:20–21

Mom just wanted the best for her boys. But can we really believe the boys hadn't thought it through long before Mom made her move? No doubt they'd been harboring feelings of inferiority, felt a bit lesser than the others, perhaps because they came from a lowly fishing family. In any case, now it was time to get their share of the pie, a place of honor in the kingdom.

Yet Jesus' rebuke is mild, filled with compassion. That's what so impresses me. For he knows human frailty, theirs and ours. "Gentlemen, I'm afraid you just don't know what you're asking," says Jesus, in effect. "Besides, in my kingdom, things are a bit topsy-turvy. Here the first will be last. And, if anybody wants to be truly great . . . well, he'll have to become a servant, the slave of all."

Graced by Affection

I'm not proud of the thoughts I harbored on that Sunday morning in the church office. But at least I let Jeff in on them a bit, enough for him to stun me with his achingly sincere response: "You know, Gary, I'm always telling people back home about my minister brother. I'm proud of you." We sat staring at each other for a few moments in awkward silence, as the little church continued to heat up.

I don't know if it's possible for siblings not to compete. I think we'll always have one eye on the other's home and car—and even children, for goodness' sake!—and secretly tabulate the supposed success ratios. But I do take comfort in knowing that something deeper than our petty covetings reverberates just under the surface.

I wish I could hear that rumbling of mutual affection more often. No doubt it is my responsibility to cultivate it, and I fail. But at least I heard it years ago in a sweaty little church office suffused with heat, light, jealousy, and love.

Adding to the Mix

We can have no relationship of depth or authenticity if we insist there is nothing wrong with us, or that it is always the other person's fault. . . . To refuse to take responsibility and admit our flaws makes the intimacy and love we seek in relationships an impossibility.

—*Rebecca Manley Pippert, writer*

Our envy of others devours us most of all.

—*Alexander Solzhenitsyn, Russian author and historian*

For the Week Ahead with Jesus

Are you out of touch with a sibling (or, if you don't have a sibling, a onetime close friend) at the moment? Are you less close than you would wish? Why not pick up the phone and call this week? Try to reconnect.

It might help to do an imagination exercise first. Quietly recall a time of conflict or bitterness that occurred between you and your brother or sister. Go back to those moments and feel the pain, jealousy, resentment. Let those feelings come flooding back for a few moments. Then imagine Jesus walking up to you both. See how he enters the scene, and spend time filling out the details.

What does he look like?

What is his facial expression?

Open your heart to Jesus and see what he does and says in the scene. Then, if so moved, pray: "Jesus, please come into this relationship between me and my sibling. Bring your healing and joy to us both."

6. When your family really needs you . . .

Just Add Jesus

"I love to sing."

I could tell just by the sparkle in his eyes and the tremor in his voice as he said those four simple words: He *adored* singing; he lived and breathed it. Song was lodged deep in my friend Larry's soul, so I'll let him tell it. . . .

I've sung leading roles in operas and soloed professionally in oratorios and in church choirs. One day, a voice teacher told me, "You have a beautiful voice—if you work with me, I know you will be doing major solos on the oratorio circuit in Chicago within two years."

I was ecstatic. I drove away from that voice lesson singing an aria from *Rigoletto* at the top of my lungs. I must have been quite a sight speeding down the Eisenhower Expressway with head thrown back, mouth wide open, gesturing wildly amidst the traffic. Okay, I was a fairly common

sight—but this wasn't another case of freak-out road rage. It was absolute spiritual bliss. I would build a career in voice!

Oh, it would mean being gone from home four or five evenings a week, plus Saturdays and Sundays. But I could do it!

Then, looming up in my mind like gentle and smiling specters, came the faces of my three lovely girls.

Up to that point, my wife, Juanita, and I had made a commitment to be with them while they were growing up. I left my office job on time most days so I could help Lori complete her butter-tub miniature golf course in the back-yard or take Reyna on a bike ride or go sledding with Joanna. But how could I be with the kids if I was forty miles away in the big city every night of the week? How would I teach them, encourage them, *father* them? And it seemed like a God-thing too: *You, Almighty, don't you want me to develop the talent with which you have so clearly gifted me?*

Where Should I Be?

Have you ever been caught in the bind between a dream and a family? Maybe you're there right now. If so, how do you know which course to take? How do you balance the call to develop your gifts—reach your vocational potential—and the seem-ingly competing call to be more of a "family person"?

It's no small question either, so please don't gloss over it too lightly. Take a moment. Breathe deeply, and feel the undercur-rents of your life flowing deep. We really are talking about your *life* here—what it is about you that makes getting up in the morning a good thing to do. Think carefully about the talents you look forward to exercising in any given day, doing the thing that feels like *the reason you were put here on earth,* that thing that brings satisfaction—and occasional exhilaration.

Now consider: Are you *allowed* to do that thing? If not, how does your life become then?

"I was *made* for this" says the one who uses his skills to the limit. Or, "I would pay *them* to let me do this job," she says. The secret longing of us all is to find that place and revel in it. If you don't believe it, consider the implausibility of . . .

Michael Jordan having never picked up a basketball in his entire life—too busy pursuing a career in hotel management.

Martin Scorsese growing up and growing old in a place where they didn't have movie theaters—teaching college math instead.

Paul McCartney never learning to play the guitar—becoming a boxing coach.

Picasso eventually retiring from life as a tour guide.

Wouldn't something always have been missing in such lives, the ache of something crucial to creaturehood but never satisfied? What specific ache would it be (or is it) for you? On the one hand, a modern-day spiritual writer like Joseph

Campbell can say that we should "follow our bliss" here on earth. On the other hand, listen to an ancient preacher . . .

Be imitators of God, therefore, as dearly loved children and live a life of love, just as Christ loved us and gave himself up for us as a fragrant offering and sacrifice to God.

Ephesians 5:1–2

What a bind for a guy like Larry and almost all of us. *Me or the ones I love?* And if I don't take care of myself first, will I really have anything within me to give away to others?

After all, they tell you on the airplane just before takeoff, "If the oxygen masks come down, put your own mask on first, and then put them on your children." Why? Because you can't help your kids breathe if you've already fainted from your own lack of O_2. So you look to your own needs first. You must be a healthy self to ensure their selves. Doesn't the principle hold when it comes to healthy *being?*

And since we're exploring the chemical reactions when adding Jesus to the "test tube of life," we've got to stop here and ask ourselves, What would Jesus contribute to the mix? Here's a little sermon he once preached . . .

The master went away on a journey, leaving his servants with his property. To one servant he gave $5 million, to another he gave $2 million, and to another, $1 million.

The first two servants invested the money while the master was away. The other took his allotted one million and kept it in a safe under his bed. When the master returned, it was judgment day:

> ✑ After a long time the master of those servants returned and settled accounts with them. . . . Then the man who had received the one [million] came. "Master," he said, "I knew that you are a hard man, harvesting where you have not sown and gathering where you have not scattered seed. So I was afraid and went out and hid your [money] in the ground. See, here is what belongs to you."
>
> His master replied, "You wicked, lazy servant!"
>
> —Matthew 25:14–19, 24–26

What if burying your best talents were like burying money in your mattress, where it can do no one any good? Please realize that I am not attempting to resolve the struggle for you in this short chapter. It is the conflict of life, and for many of us, it may not be resolved until after life. However, I do invite you to think, What would it mean for me, in the midst of family responsibilities, to try to please Jesus with the gifts he's given me?

Larry Stayed Home

According to Larry, "That night some twenty-five years ago—the very same day when I reveled in my expressway ecstasy—I decided to give up singing at a competitive level so I could be with my wife and our children. Yet to *this* day

I think about *that* day. Maybe I should have gone for it, followed my dream. Maybe if I had, I'd be famous.

"I'm not saying I was a perfect father, either. But not long ago, I received a letter from Joanna, who has grown up and is living on her own now. She wrote,

❧ Dear Daddy,
I thank you for raising me to believe I have valuable resources within me. I really feel I can do anything. This is a gift I am eternally grateful for, and I know I am blessed to have been given such a father. I love you.

Joanna

So Larry chose not to make a career out of his singing. But that certainly didn't mean his gifted voice went unused or was buried in any way. In fact, it was just a week or so ago that I sat in a beautiful church sanctuary in sunlit stillness, with incense perfuming the air, my soul imbibing the most glorious rendition of *Panis Angelicus, Fit Panis Hominum*. The voice was Larry's. But the words felt as if sprinkled down from heaven into my heart . . .

❧ Bread of angels is made the Bread of man—
Living Bread from heaven:
O wondrous gift!
The Lord gives Himself
To the poor and the humble. . . .

Lead us in your way,
that we at last may see
the light wherein you dwell.

At that moment I was, indeed, enlightened by an idea: It must be a significant offense when Jesus gives us a gift and we don't even *try* to use it. We *may* not make a career of it; we *must* not make a coffin for it.

In the meantime, the family keeps calling . . .

Adding to the Mix

Do not grow weary of doing little things for the love of God, who looks not on the great size of the work, but on the love in it.

> —Practice of the Presence of God,
> *by Brother Lawrence,*
> *Seventeenth-century Carmelite*
> *lay brother and author*

Work is not primarily a thing one does to live, but the thing one lives to do. It is, or should be, the full expression of the worker's faculties, the thing in which he finds spiritual, mental, and bodily satisfaction.

> —Dorothy Sayers, novelist

For the Week Ahead with Jesus

Contact a friend who will set a time to go over your last performance review, or your work goals (sales quota or project objectives, etc.) for the coming year. Ask him or her to help you analyze your skill at balancing work and family demands.

The point is to bring in an objective observer who can help you answer questions like these:

- How realistic is my manager in asking me to accomplish these things?

- How much time and energy have these kinds of goals required (or will they require) of me?

- How well have I been able to reserve time and energy for my family while pursuing these standards at work?

- If Jesus were my supervisor, what legitimate adjustments to my "drive to produce" might he ask me to consider?

One of the most unique things about Jesus was his approach to conquering the world. Normally, as you scan the pages of history, you see the conquerors standing out with some rather unique personalities, and all kinds of distinctive political theories, but very little creativity when it comes to the taking-over part.

In fact, that part is quite predictable. Bring out the archers first. Launch wave after wave of arrows into the sky (how often do we hear the ancients speaking of "blotting out the sun" with their missiles?). Then call up the cavalry. Make charge after charge, hoping to ride down the enemy. The more ambitious individuals would attach swords or razor-sharp scythes to their chariot-wheel axels in hopes of shredding any slow-footed combatants (the lack of mobility, though, usually made these monstrosities a liability; ranks of foot

fighters would simply step aside and spear the hapless drivers from behind). Then, finally, send in the infantry for the hand-to-hand carnage deciding the fate of a people, at least for the near future.

You see it from Xerxes to Alexander, from Napoleon to Hitler. Strategies and tactics vary little; it's just the hardware that changes.

Force.

Firepower.

Overwhelming numbers.

These have been the keys to success.

And please do accept my assertion that Jesus was indeed a world conqueror. To this day, he claims over 2 billion subjects across the globe, with no flash-in-the-pan, short-term reign. So he's been successful.

But now let's get back to the truly astounding thing: his methods. He chose to start his campaign not with the biggest army around, but with the smallest entity that can still be called a group—three men.

He chose three men to get close to: Peter, James, and John.

That's it. That's the essence of the plan, the totality of the strategy. If you want to talk tactics, then we could add this to round things out: He told the men that his leadership flow-chart would go from bottom to top, not vice versa. Power would be given away rather than hoarded. Or, as he put it to the group as it grew a little bigger, "From now on, I'll just be your servant—here, let me wash your feet . . . so you'll know how to wash each other's" (read about it in John 13:1–38).

Eventually, the group became twelve mentorees, then seventy-two. But with those initial three, Jesus started a discipline process that ended up transforming the terrestrial landscape. All his waking hours involved giving his life to these guys. Pouring his own being into them. Telling them what he knew, what he thought, what he desired. Praying with them, showing them his priorities, demonstrating his power, conveying his working principles.

In short, he opened up his heart to them, and in the process these men saw glory. Heaven was revealed along with heaven-on-earth as it could be. They were caught, inspired, encouraged, and released to be what he had been to others. He left them to do battle with love and grace as the prime weapons—to be his mouth and hands and feet in the world.

In the Bible, the Book of Acts shows what the disciples were able to accomplish simply by having been with Jesus for three short years. I'll let their contemporaries say it: "These men have turned the world upside down!" (see Acts 17:6).

What a Role Model!

He had a bushy shock of white hair—and his unusual name only highlighted it: Rev. Forest Bush. He was my first mentor in ministry, and to me that white hair stood for exactly what it has traditionally come to symbolize: wisdom.

I was young, just out of Bible school, not even started in seminary. But this wise district pastor saw me as capable, believing that my early twenty-something enthusiasm would offset whatever I lacked in formal training. I was to take a tiny church on partial pay and continue with seminary after a couple of years "in the trenches." And I did, indeed, approach the task with all the vigor and idealism I could muster . . . before soon slipping deeply into the mire of discouragement.

The thing I remember about Forest, though, was that in his visits or in our phone conversations, he was always accepting, gently encouraging, constantly telling me how things would be as soon as we "turned the corner" with the church. He was my overseer, but he never lorded it over me, not once. He just had no concept of power games.

After six months, when I phoned to report that not one single new member had yet entered the church—and I was horrified at my apparent pastoral failure—Forest was not in the least disturbed. "Just keep on loving those people," he said. "They have so much talent and ability; let them use it." As far as he was concerned, this little church would be a great one before too long . . . he could virtually see it.

Amazingly, I began to see it, too. I caught his vision as though it had been a baseball tossed from his mitt to mine.

Why did I begin to put so much stock in the words of this man who was decades my senior? For one thing, while house-sitting for him one evening, I came across a scrapbook on his bookshelf. I opened it to an old snapshot of Forest as a young minister, probably about my age at the time. Was he standing in a pulpit preaching to a tiny flock? No. Was he presiding over a wedding or a funeral? No, not in the one old Polaroid that has left such an impression in my mind all these years.

Instead, there was Forest atop a bulldozer, triumphant smile on his face, mounds of broken-up mortar, bricks, boards, and shingles cluttering the background. That rubble had once housed the blossoming numbers of his first pastorate, a congregation that—as he told me later—had far outgrown its old building under brand-new sermons.

It was everything I needed to keep going. Rev. Bush had been there, he knew what could happen. He had been a part of it, happily bulldozing old bricks while claiming new vistas for the Lord. And the vision he gave me was the glimpse of a future so sure and so certain that I felt I could reach out and touch it. It was like broken plaster and bits of torn-up carpet in the palm of my hand.

Looking for That Visionary?

When were you provided vision from someone older and wiser than you? Or are you looking for that influence these days and maybe having some trouble finding it?

There is nothing like being grasped by a wise mentor's vision. So I hope you will stay alert for that special, humble human being who will spark your vision and take you alongside. And if you have not tried him yet, I highly recommend Jesus for the job. He is still conquering the universe, still in the mentoring business, and still calling each one of us, "that at the name of Jesus every knee should bow, in heaven and on earth and under the earth" (Philippians 2:10). You can hardly go wrong in adding his wisdom to your life—and emulating his methods.

The awesome thing to contemplate is that we most certainly will—all of us—bend our knees in obeisance to this mighty lord. The only question is, When?

Adding to the Mix

The visions that we present to our [younger generation] shape the future. They become self-fulfilling prophecies. Dreams are maps.

—Carl Sagan, novelist

Our young people need to know we have discovered the seeds of greatness within them. When they finally find someone who recognizes their potential, they will abandon the direction this world has given them. When they see an older generation that is convinced of their potential, there is nothing they won't do to fulfill that potential.

—Inspire the Fire,
by Ron Luce, youth minister

The tenders of vision are often lonely, usually unpopular, and frequently demand that others change. People with a vision inject ambiguity and risk and uncertainty into our lives.

—Leadership Jazz,
by Max De Pree, international church consultant

For the Week Ahead with Jesus

During a time of quiet this week, take a moment to think about the importance of vision and who is helping you find it. First, if you keep a journal, jot the names of a few people around you that you admire, perhaps from a distance. Who among them might make a good mentor for you? What could you do to approach that person with your idea?

Second, jot the name of a young man or young woman in whom you see potential—either in the work environment or in your neighborhood. Look for an opportunity to let this person know what you see in him or her.

*I*n 1970, cartoonist Mel Lazarus developed the popular comic strip *Momma,* about an older widow. Momma has a perpetual suitor, a strange man named Mr. K.

He's really not much of a catch, but he is certainly a hanger-on. In one strip, as the two elderly folks sit in the living room together, Mr. K. says, "Mrs. Hobbs, I am at a low ebb, psychologically. My ego is flattened." Mrs. Hobbs responds, "Mr. K., let me hasten to state that you're a fine, interesting and attractive man."

Mr. K.'s face brightens perceptibly and he pursues the issue: "Oh, Mrs. Hobbs, is that the truth?"

Mrs. Hobbs answers, "No. There'll be plenty of time for the truth when you're emotionally stronger." In considering masks, it's helpful to ask these questions:

◆ How do you decide who is "safe," and who isn't, for a deeper level of vulnerability in a relationship? (Do you just let everybody know "where you are," like Mr. K.?)

◆ Where do you draw the line between legitimate sharing of personal struggles and inappropriate "airing of dirty laundry"?

◆ Isn't it a relief to finally remove the mask?

I was in the car with Phil when he suddenly pulled to the curb, apparently wanting to talk. I was glad, because as a young minister, I wanted to develop a mentoring relationship with this college student. Accepting a ride from him seemed to be the opening for significant conversation.

But he surprised me by blurting a speech, reeling off the words as though previously memorized: "Gary, I'm usually kind of nervous in relating with people, afraid of what they'll think of me, but I have a theory that if I tell a person—right off—the absolute worst thing about me, then I can relax and be free because I'll have nothing to hide from then on."

I was just beginning to reply that it was an interesting concept when he broke in with, "Well, here goes. Anyway, I have this problem with sexual lust, see. I secretly buy a lot of those skin magazines and spend lots of time fantasizing, then I throw 'em away and buy some more. It actually gets pretty expensive, though I suppose you wouldn't think about me that way, but it's the truth and nobody knows it, I mean, except for you, now."

He smiled at me triumphantly, because a big load was off his chest and he was presumably now "free" not to worry about what I thought of him. The shocker came in my realization that *it was now supposed to be my turn*. With expectant eyes drilling into mine, everything in his body language beckoned, "Okay, go . . . So what's the absolute worst, Gary? I can handle it. Go ahead."

I chickened out. Actually, I could have told any number of true, down-to-earth stories of similar struggles with lust— and a few other not-so-nice peccadilloes. But, after all, I was his spiritual leader. *And where does he get off thinking that I, too, am some kind of gross sinner?*

I said something appropriately pastoral: "That's good, Phil, being able to share with me like that; it took some courage, I'll be praying for you." Or something like that. When you offer a proper generalization in these situations, the words don't really matter; what matters is that you shut down the dialogue, close off the relationship—quick.

Should I have opened up to Phil with a reciprocal level of transparency?

I played it a bit holier than that. The thing is, I can't remember another significant talk with the young man during the rest of my years in that church.

And suppose Jesus had entered that conversation between Phil and me? I want to delve into that deeply, even now after so many years have passed. But first, there's a philosophical issue to settle. Here's what I mean: If Jesus already knows us completely—all we've ever done or will do, and even what we're thinking—why does he call us to reveal ourselves to him, confess our sins to him, approach him in all transparency? Isn't it an exercise in redundancy?

Maybe not. Could it be that there is a real and vast difference between God knowing us and our choice to unveil before him? I think of my twins when they were toddlers. I would watch one of them pick up a piece of candy that he'd been told he couldn't have. Yes, I knew what was in his hand, but I would ask, "What's that in your hand, Tim?"

Then I'd wait expectantly.

Hoping he'd choose to show me.

Or would he turn and run away?

Is that how it is when Jesus asks us to open up to him? The point, I'm beginning to realize, is that all the ways Jesus works with us in our relationship together are for *our* benefit, for *our* growth as spiritual beings. It is for us to grow in the humility of this self-revealing before him. Yes, he knows us, and he invites *us* to know us, along with him in the relationship.

For it is the relationship with him that counts above all else. Beyond all attempts at good living or keeping the rules, knowing him—dwelling with him in the moment-by-moment of our days—that's what matters. And how can we enjoy a deep relationship if we bring a false self to it?

That, then, is the philosophical question and my attempt to answer it. So, I search my heart in my times of quiet and ask, What rooms within me still have locks on the doors?

What would it take for me to dare to open those doors a crack and let myself, with Jesus' arm around me, take a glimpse inside? And what would that glimpse call me to *feel* or to *change* or to *do* in light of full disclosure?

When Jesus Looks at the Inside

On a hot and dusty day in century one, a religious leader named Simon asked Jesus to eat with him. So Jesus went into the man's house and took his place at the table. But a woman, a surprise to both of the men, also soon enters the house, a loose woman carrying a jar of ointment.

Without a word, this woman of dubious reputation goes to Jesus, bends down before him, and begins washing his feet . . . with her *tears.* She dries his feet with her hair and kisses them continually.

She says nothing. Or does she?

The religious man is thinking, If this young preacher was actually a prophet, he'd know the type of woman he's entertaining at the moment—and he'd kick her out *now!*

Okay, so we have a silent woman speaking with her humble actions, and a silent religionist speaking to himself with his prideful thoughts. And then Jesus speaks . . .

> "Simon, I have something to say to you."
>
> "Teacher," he replied, "Speak."
>
> "A certain creditor had two debtors; one owed five hundred denarii, and the other fifty. When they could not pay, he canceled

the debts for both of them. Now which of them will love him more?"

Simon answered, "I suppose the one for whom he canceled the greater debt." And Jesus said to him, "You have judged rightly."

Then turning toward the woman, he said to Simon, "Do you see this woman? I entered your house; you gave me no water for my feet, but she has bathed my feet with her tears and dried them with her hair. You gave me no kiss, but from the time I came in she has not stopped kissing my feet. You did not anoint my head with oil, but she has anointed my feet with ointment. Therefore, I tell you, her sins, which were many, have been forgiven; hence she has shown great love. But the one to whom little is forgiven, loves little."

Then he said to her, "Your sins are forgiven."
—Luke 7:40–48 (New Revised Standard Version)

It appears that humble self-revelation, like the loose woman's undisguised affection for Jesus, has its benefits. It is excruciatingly difficult and inconvenient. But it gets heavenly attention and leads to significant change. *And it is called a form of love.*

Then again, Jesus can be a pretty safe choice when it comes to revealing one's sins, love, humility, or desire for repentance. We can surely open our hearts wide to him. But we still face the big question: To what degree shall I reveal my "true self" to the one sitting next to me today?

When I think of brutal honesty, I recall the story about the candid dentist who was overheard speaking to his patient as he bends over him with a hypodermic needle in hand: "You might feel a little sting. On the other hand, it might feel as though you've been kicked in the mouth by a mule."

In other words, it's much better in some cases to hold back a bit. Yes, find a special friend, a spiritual director, or even a small group that, over the years, has become a safe place for such personal sharing.

But don't share with everyone! Not casual acquaintances or untested ministers. Bearing our souls to some folks is like putting out fresh meat for a pack of wolves. We'll come back from the experience seriously wounded, if not soul dead.

So, how do I add Jesus here? It has to do with an opening of the heart to a place we'd prefer to keep closed. I know what that feels like for me, but I can't tell you exactly what it is like for you. But *you* know. To get a feel for it, just recall the various times in your relationships when you felt a powerful "nudge" to let down, to give in, open up. Then didn't two equally powerful forces—like battling beasts—suddenly began a titanic struggle within you? One was a horrific fear; the other was a glorious glimpse of a possibility of wholeness and freedom—a fleeting possibility that could only come at the price of a determined letting go . . .

- ◆ You have a brief, minor argument with a friend. It's over, and there is a moment of silence in which the relationship can go either way . . . if only someone would say, *"Hey, I guess I was wrong about. . . ."*

◆ You've just been turned down for sex by a tired spouse. You turn to the other side of the bed, close down the conversation, and think, *But wouldn't it be better if I turned back around and said something kind before we go to sleep?*

◆ You face a rebellious teenage son who once again smarts off with a wisecrack. You lay into him with a few cracks of your own (instead of trying to uncover the real problem). Later, he comes up to apologize, and you'd like to hug him, *but your arms feel stiff and don't move.*

In each of those situations—that is, in the similar, but unique ones in your own life—just ask yourself, *What was the thing that held me back? What was it that kept me from reaching out?*

Your answer will help you grasp the thing that keeps your mask firmly in place. Take that thing out, let it go, and the mask, too, will begin to loosen. It may even fall clean away.

Adding to the Mix

No one, for any considerable period, can wear one face to himself, and another to the multitude, without finally getting bewildered as to which may be the true.

—*Nathaniel Hawthorne, nineteenth-century novelist*

How often we hide behind masks . . . In the nearness of real, deep, substantial love we run back to our masks of isolation, shallowness, and safety in terror of being revealed and accepted. We hide ourselves in acts of passion; we buy love under false prudence; we substitute biological pleasures for the divine wonder and peril of love; we surround ourselves with cold, icy barriers to defend the smug self from being shattered by love.

—Art of Being Human,
by William McNamara, British mystic

Before God can deliver us from ourselves we must un-deceive ourselves.
—*St. Augustine*

For the Week Ahead with Jesus

During the coming week, think through your relationships. Consider:

- Which of these relationships is safe for me to go deeper into self-revelation? Why?

- Which of my relationships must, for safety reasons, remain somewhat superficial?

- When it comes to my relationship with Jesus at the moment, how self-revealing have I been? Why? What next step would I like to take in this area?

*I*n Chapter 8 we discussed the humble unveiling of a human heart—to the people around us and to Jesus. In this chapter, we go a step further to consider, What, exactly, do we unveil when we expose our faith? Do the folks around us see actions that support our words? Ideally, removing the mask on our religion will reveal something solid, something downright genuine.

Not easy to accomplish, though.

Lawrence, missionary kid and cross-cultural trainer, told me about balancing his oversized Samsonite on one shoulder, staggering up the trail, and gasping in the thin Himalayan air.

✑ When I reached our cottage, I swung the suitcase to the ground and cried, "I'm home!" I had thought about this moment constantly during the three weeks I had been away—the moment when I would see my family again. We were living in northern India for six months while I led religious writers' workshops throughout Asia. My mission, working as a cross-cultural publishing consultant for a Christian foundation, was to assist local churches to produce their own literature. The past weeks had been particularly arduous. After ten-hour days of training, the young people always insisted I join them on moonlight walks for long discussions on life, culture, the Bible, world religions—anything at all. I loved them all, and I hoped that just as their lives enriched me, so my teaching and example would encourage and edify them.

But now, I thought, *it's time for my wife, Juanita, to fall adoringly at my feet. And my three daughters will climb on me, too, and offer me fresh fruit. . . .*

It was nothing like that.

When I opened the door of the cottage, the children were nowhere to be found. And Juanita, after visiting with me briefly, suggested I "get some rest" while she ran to a meeting. She would see me later for dinner; if not, "just heat something up."

I was furious. I made some sarcastic comment and tossed my suitcase on the bed. Then I wrote a venomous note and charged out to wander alone along mountain trails, throwing stones and muttering to myself until well after dark.

When I returned, I stopped on the trail, ashamed and frightened of myself, and peered down at the lights of our cottage below. *What kind of person am I, to change so quickly from spiritual leader to petty, self-centered child?*

Juanita and I talked the next day. I admitted my selfishness and apologized. No, life did not revolve around me, and yes, life went on with the family even when I returned home. This didn't mean we loved each other any less.

The whole episode, though, illustrated to me once again what a struggle it has been for me to walk that razor-thin path between genuine and hollow faith.

I asked Lawrence to go back to that cottage in his mind for a moment. To go back, be there in his anger, tossing his suitcase, and *imagine Jesus standing in the corner.* How would it change the environment? He thought about it for a long moment, then said, "'I will have mercy and not sacrifice.' That's what I hear Jesus saying to me."

It is something Jesus said while here on earth, on at least two occasions. In the first instance, Jesus was sitting at a meal in a tax-collector's house. Many somewhat questionable people were there with him, people you might not want your daughter to date too seriously. (Matthew, the tax collector who was hosting the event, had apparently invited many of his friends to the dinner so they could meet Jesus.)

But when certain *very* religious folks (known as Pharisees) looked in the window and saw this strange gathering of a preacher hanging out with a bunch of sinners, they couldn't take it. They just had to say something. That's when Jesus told them, "It is not the healthy who need a doctor, but the sick. But go and learn what this means: 'I desire mercy, not sacrifice.' For I have not come to call the righteous, but sinners" (Matthew 9:13).

On the second occasion, Jesus was walking outside with his disciples when everybody got hungry. Since they happened to be traveling through a farmer's field, his friends decided to start picking the heads of grain for a little dry-cereal snack. Big problem! Why? Two reasons: those very religious people were watching again (yep, the ever-present rival, that Pharisee crowd) and the day of the week was Saturday. The Pharisees had strict rules about what could be done on the Sabbath day, and picking grain was a definite no-no.

So, Jesus responded to them once again. Among other things, he said, "Haven't you read in the Law that on the Sabbath the priests in the temple desecrate the day and yet are innocent? I tell you that one greater than the temple is here. If you had known what these words mean, 'I desire mercy, not sacrifice,' you would not have condemned the innocent. For the Son of Man is Lord of the Sabbath" (Matthew 12:5–8).

It's a concise, thoroughly intriguing statement that makes us wish we could know exactly what he meant—*I want mercy, not sacrifice.* What does it speak to your heart?

I hear it like this: "Gary, I'm *always* standing in the corner of your days. I'm *always* there with you, in every event. So, be sure that when you are choosing how to act, you consider *the whole room*—the total environment, with all the beating hearts around you—and all the possibilities, especially how what you are about to do or say will be for . . . others."

I'm thinking that what God desires far more than our ritual goodness (our type of employment? our sacrificial religious discipline? our accomplishments? our church attendance?) is kindness of spirit. The sacrifice of a true heart, one full of mercy for others.

That's it. The only thing left for me to glean, then, is how "Gary" would look, living continually in this mercy mode. That is, for example, when I face the kind of homecoming friction that Lawrence described in his Himalayan story, how would I do things differently if my faith was *genuine* rather than *hollow* at just those moments?

The bottom line comes through to me from religious writer William Barclay in the most direct and helpful terms, so I'll leave you with his words: "What God desires far more than ritual sacrifice is . . . the spirit which knows no law other than that it must answer the call of human need." (By the way, another missionary, E. Stanley Jones, said that a Hindu once commented to him, "I am not enamored by your dramatic gestures. If you have found Christ, tell us simply and straightforwardly.")

Adding to the Mix

Do not merely listen to the word, and so deceive yourselves. Do what it says. Anyone who listens to the word but does not do what it says is like a man who looks at his face in a mirror and, after looking at himself, goes away and immediately forgets what he looks like.

—James 1:22–24

Oh, I don't reject your Christ. I love your Christ. It's just that so many of you Christians are so unlike your Christ.

—*Mahatma Gandhi*

For the Week Ahead with Jesus

During the week, do some more thinking about the "gap" between belief and action in your life. Choose a response:

Typically, in my life . . .
a.   I do more than I know.
b.   I know more than I do.

If you chose b, what area of theological knowledge needs more shoe leather attached to it? You may find it helpful to write down the idea on a piece of paper.

10. When you're weary of rescuing (or being rescued) . . .

Just Add Jesus

*O*nce again we'd fallen into the same marital battle that escalated along well-worn paths of pain and confusion. Here's how it goes: She's being mistreated at work. I listen, telling myself that this time I will only play the role of comforter and encourager. But the reports of unfairness and apparent injustice light my fuse. I get angry and want to protect her; I'll do anything to make her life all right again. But, once again, she thinks I'm angry at her. *No! You don't understand; I'm just angry about what's happening to you. . . .*

Deep inside, I sense that all she wants is a listening ear and a little comfort. But I feel wired to protect, driven to solve her problem:

"You should have said this . . ."
"You could have done that . . ."
"Why don't you . . . ?"

Why can't I let her have her own life? Isn't she allowed to have problems and struggles, too, just like me? I've grown through facing adversity, haven't I? Why can't I allow my wife the same privilege? Besides, who made me responsible to make everything okay, anyway?

Somehow, for me, it all connects back to the day of my father's funeral, when, as we slowly followed the casket into the church, I took my grandfather's words deeply to heart, as the truth of my life: "Get up there and *take care of your mother*. You're the man of the house now."

It's not unusual to hear words like that. It seems to be an ancient tradition. In fact, there's a Bible story that reveals man's long-standing tendency to fix woman. It all comes through in the four short chapters of the Book of Ruth.

Ruth became one of Jesus' "mothers"; that is, one of the women listed in the gospels as an ancestor, a human contributor to Jesus' human nature. If I may digress for a moment here, I'd like to point out that Jesus' having this human line of ancestors is crucial to his person and mission on earth and now in heaven. You see, Jesus is the God-Man, and he had to have two natures in one person in order to be the savior of the world. Think about it. All of the New Testament writers who tell us about his reason for coming to earth stress his sacrificial work. Now, a sacrifice on behalf of others, when it is a religious accomplishment with real effects, has two prime requirements: First, the one sacrificed must thoroughly represent the ones who will benefit. Second, the sacrifice, if it is to convey a true salvation—an *eternal* salvation, as the Bible claims it to be—must be an *eternal* sacrifice.

Can you see, then, why Jesus would have to be fully human in order to be fully representative of humans, and why he would have to be fully eternal God in order to make the sacrifice an eternally effective one?

Now, back to Ruth, a grandmother of Jesus in the long line of his human antecedents, a young girl who lived many centuries before Baby Jesus entered his Bethlehem manger. She entered as a foreigner-widow into Israel and would have had a very hard time finding a new husband, except that her mother-in-law, Naomi, spied a potential mate for her in a man named Boaz. To make a long story short, the two met, and things progressed rapidly. For our purposes, we can pick up the relationship between Ruth and Boaz right here . . .

[Ruth] exclaimed, "Why have I found such favor in your eyes that you notice me—a foreigner?"

Boaz replied, "I've been told all about what you have done for your mother-in-law since the death of your husband—how you left your father and mother and your homeland and came to live with a people you did not know before. May the LORD repay you for what you have done. May you be richly rewarded by the LORD, the God of Israel, under whose wings you have come to take refuge."

"May I continue to find favor in your eyes, my lord," she said. "You have given me comfort and have spoken kindly to your servant—though I do not have the standing of one of your servant girls."

At mealtime Boaz said to her, "Come over here. Have some bread and dip it in the wine vinegar." When she sat down with the harvesters, he offered her some roasted grain. She ate all she wanted and had some left over. As she got up to glean, Boaz gave orders to his men, "Even if she gathers among the sheaves, don't embarrass her. Rather, pull out some stalks for her from the bundles and leave them for her to pick up, and don't rebuke her."

". . . And now, my daughter, don't be afraid. *I will do for you all you ask.*"

—Ruth 2:10–16; 3:11 (Italics added)

One big thing he did was offer himself to her for marriage. But my interest here is Boaz's all-encompassing, I'll-fix-things-for-you-don't-worry statement to Ruth. I'm wondering what some of the effects of making the kind of promise he makes to Ruth might be.

And suppose it's a kind of promise that's fully inbred in the male psyche (though hardly available to our everyday consciousness) and kicks into play automatically?

"I *must* solve her problem," we think.

And why not? A man is taught to be a problem solver, a helper, a fixer, a hero, a rescuer of women. On the one hand, this can be a good thing—we see Ruth eating when she's hungry. But it quickly turns excessive. You see, someone playing this fixer role requires the other person to play the role of the problem person, the helpee, the broken, the vanquished, the wounded.

Just for Male Readers . . .

Truth to tell, I enjoy being the knight in shining armor. And there's surely a legitimate place for manly leadership and protection. But suppose this role-playing were gradually transformed a bit? Maybe some new lines of honest communication could open, if I were occasionally released from the hero role and allowed off the pedestal, right?

Just for Female Readers . . .

I [Gary] invited my wife, Carol, to address you here . . . "When I share my problems, how people are mistreating me at work, or how somebody yelled at me in a meeting, there's only one thing I want: *empathy*. That comes through in attentive listening and warm touch. Period. If I wanted somebody to tell me how to act differently, or how to learn assertiveness, or how to do it next time, well, maybe I'd go to a counselor and learn. Nope, I want a husband, somebody who can put his arm around me and say, 'That must have been tough; how did you feel?' Then, just be quiet and let me drink in your caring."

• • •

Okay. So far we've connected to Jesus indirectly, remotely, only by means of genealogy and by referring to his ancestry in Ruth. But is there a way to add him, too, to the marital struggle here?

Problem is, Jesus was never married. But he plays the role of woman rescuer in one incident that appears in three of the Gospels: A woman plagued by abnormal menstrual bleeding for twelve years comes and touches Jesus' cloak. The text in Mark 5:25-34 conveys five facts making things crystal clear to me:

> *The woman assumed she could be healed just by a touch;*
> *Jesus felt power go out of him at her touch;*
> *He embraced her problem without actively trying to solve it;*
> *He related gently, with an endearing word: "Daughter";*
> *He allowed something within her to do all the "work" necessary:*
> *"Daughter, your faith has healed you. Go in peace and be freed from*
> *your suffering."*

What blessed words to hear! So, woman needing help . . . comes to man . . . experiences touch . . . hears an endearing word . . . is allowed to heal herself. I can work with that.

Adding to the Mix

We [men] cast others, especially women, in follower roles, because we are cast in leader roles. Then we coach them to be good followers and diagnose bad following as a problem. Neither of us wants this when we stop to think about it.

—The Male Predicament:
On Being a Man Today, *by James Dittes*

Years ago, manhood was an opportunity for achievement, and now it is a problem to be overcome. . . . [But] we are lovers and artists and adventurers, meant to be noble, free-ranging, and foolish, like dogs, not competing for a stamp of approval: "Friend of Womanhood."
> —The Book of Guys, *by Garrison Keillor*

For the Week Ahead with Jesus

For Men

Do some thinking about these questions during the week: In what specific situations is it legitimate for me to be the knight in shining armor—hero, protector, rescuer? And when does playing that role make others into the vanquished? On a piece of paper, make yourself two columns: "Times for knighthood" and "Times to remove the armor." Jot ideas in each column.

For Women

Jot some responses:

- If I were given a chance to tell men what women want and need, how would I say it?

- What are some ways of attempting to heal myself that will also let man in—in an affirming way?

I awoke to a bright, beautiful day. I heard birds chirping, saw fluffy clouds passing as I looked out the bedroom window. As soon as I discovered my shirtsleeve button missing, though, my mood took a downward turn. *Why am I still wearing this same old crummy shirt?* I thought. *Isn't it about time I got some new clothes, anyway? Why go around looking like an indigent?*

I couldn't find another clean shirt, and the missing button meant I'd have to go to work with my shirtsleeves rolled up! I found a needle and thread, but I couldn't seem to thread the needle. I woke my wife and pleaded with her to try to thread that crazy pygmy needle, but she couldn't do it either.

"Never mind!" I shouted, anger escalating. "I'll just go like this. But I'm telling you, one of these days I've just got to get a real suit of clothes, with a real shirt with buttons, and a tie, and a good

belt . . . and *everything*!" I kicked a pillow from the carpet and watched it rebound off the wall as I stormed out.

That's me: the man of the house. A disciple of Jesus, and thus (merely by default?) spiritual leader of the family. How do I do it? It's easy; this kind of leadership comes quite naturally to me.

It's All about What's *Not* There

So, just after I send the pillow into that wall, suppose Jesus enters. Not to scold me, necessarily, though that would be a valid option. No, suppose he walks in as a mentor, or a model, of *how I could be instead,* should he empower a transformation deep within me.

The question is, Would the transformation involve *adding* something? Would I need to brush up on the Commandments, for instance, and garner a more profound respect for God's ways? Or perhaps I could gain wisdom, insight, new principles to apply here?

But then I realize, if Jesus were to stand before me as a model of relational health and wholeness, he'd be inviting me simply to look at him and see him—not so much what is there, but what is *not* there. He would beckon me to know his mind, his attitude, his whole perspective on being a human and interacting with human beings. He would invite me to notice what is *not* there. Rather than add something to my repertoire of human relations skills, he'd ask me to lay something down.

But what?

Here is how the apostle Paul (a man who'd personally encountered Jesus and knew him well) put it in the Bible:

> ✐ Your attitude should be the same as that of Christ Jesus: Who, being in very nature God, did not consider equality with God something to be grasped, but made himself nothing, taking the very nature of a servant, being made in human likeness.
>
> And being found in appearance as a man, he humbled himself and became obedient to death—even death on a cross!
>
> —Philippians 2:5–8

Amazingly, to have the mind of Christ is to have something less than I have now:

Less ego,
Less of a need to be served,
Less of a demand to have things work to my liking.

To put it in reverse fashion, amidst this great mystery of religious growth, I must gain more emptiness.

I use the term *empty* deliberately, for it is at the heart of this Bible passage. In the original Greek language that Paul used to pen these words, *ekenosen* means "emptied" or "void." Our translation above renders the word "made himself nothing." Here is how a few other Bibles translate that word:

He "made himself of no reputation" (King James Version)
He "emptied Himself" (New American Standard Bible)
He "gave up all he had" (Good News Translation)
He "set aside the privileges of deity" (The Message)
He "gave up his place with God" (New Century Version)
He "made himself as nothing" (The Bible in Basic English)
He "stripped Himself of His glory" (Weymouth New Testament)

The basic idea is not that Jesus gave away his deity but that, in all humility, he chose not to display it openly and exercise it in its full power. Humans across time and culture have known that emptying oneself is the essence of the religious impulse. The only way to scale the heights of spirituality is to go deep—to let go, to give up. *Exinanition* (the Latin word for *ekenosen*) before exaltation.

If the use of pure willpower is the absolute opposite of genuine religious devotion, then ego relinquishment is its shining jewel. Listen to more from Jesus along these lines. . . .

"The last will be first, and the first will be last." (Matthew 20:16)

"Everyone who exalts himself will be humbled, and he who humbles himself will be exalted." (Luke 14:11)

"I tell you the truth, unless a kernel of wheat falls to the ground and dies, it remains only a single seed. But if it dies, it produces many seeds." (John 12:24)

Ego relinquishment won't save our souls, because it is a nonentity that must eventually lead us to a saving essence. But it *can* do that. And once we know the Savior, ego relinquishment can keep us going deeper and higher—in humility and servanthood—a most blessed paradox.

Now let's come back to me, the button, and the family. . . .

Family Man

Lately I've been thinking a lot about my role as a Jesus follower, the relationship between me and my Lord, and how it must appear to my family. And so often it's not a pretty picture. Of course, I have my periods of revival, when I determine to make a new start, to be a loving, Jesus-added example to my wife and kids "from now on." It never works that way for very long, though.

But maybe it's not those periods of agonizing introspection or the frequent all-or-nothing rededications that determine the quality of my discipleship in my family's eyes. It probably involves, in a more profound way, the little decisions I make each moment about how I will be around my wife and kids (or around my friends and coworkers). I face those kinds of decisions just as soon as I get out of bed, walk to the closet, and gear up for another round of spiritual battle. If only I will relax and choose the most "uncluttered" way—the path of emptying. I'm most successful when I lay down my weapons. Just yesterday, I felt anger rising within me at an insensitive remark. I felt put down, belittled. Then

I thought about the speaker for a moment, considered the pressure he's under, the tough times he's endured in recent months. I realized I could accept the remarks without having to fight back or even defend. A hole seemed to open up in my heart, a place where even unkind words could be accepted and transformed. Here was an emptiness that allowed me to move on in peace.

Adding to the Mix

The real problem of the Christian life comes where people do not usually look for it. It comes the very moment you wake up each morning. All your wishes and hopes for the day rush at you like wild animals. And the first job each morning consists simply in shoving them all back; in listening to that other voice, taking that other point of view, letting that other larger, stronger, quieter life come flowing in.

—Mere Christianity, *by C. S. Lewis*

If you are humble, nothing will touch you, neither praise nor disgrace, because you know what you are.

—Mother Teresa

Because I am God's daughter, a bridge, a path, a secret stair has been built from his heart to mine so that, by the Spirit, God's thoughts can step into my mind.

—Luci Shaw, writer

For the Week Ahead with Jesus

Maintain a daily diary of "wake-up thoughts" for one week. Keep your journal or pencil and paper next to your bed and record your first thoughts upon waking. For example, note:

- Your overall mood

- Worries and frustrations that hit you

- Desires and needs that become apparent

- Habits or patterns of thought or action that automatically take over

Evaluate your entries at the end of the week and consider, How does my wake-up routine usually affect the quality of my relationships during the rest of the day?

12. When you're dealing with a "problem person" . . .

Just Add Jesus

I was to speak at the Olive Branch Mission one Wednesday morning a few years ago. The mission sat in the heart of skid row in downtown Chicago. I remember parking my car and walking toward the entrance, where some sleepy-eyed men had gathered, waiting for the mission to open for the day. I greeted them with what I thought was a friendly voice. Yet one of the men turned to me with a vicious look and snarled out from under a ragged fedora, "Don't look down on me, sir. You may think you know what kind of person I am—but you don't. I happen to be an excellent scientist. I have a Ph.D. from Michigan State."

Did he have a doctoral degree from that big university? I have no doubt that he did. But what had happened? At some point, he had begun walking the streets, begging. Immediately I wanted to protest his assessment of my attitude . . . but I

knew I *did* look down on him at that moment. And I hated that reaction in me, my revulsion at his greasy clothes, his unwashed face, his sour odor. My automatic assumption was that he was foregoing the responsible life of an excellent scientist because he was lazy, that he somehow found homelessness *easier* than working a job.

But I was there as a compassionate ambassador of Jesus. How ironic! Even if I suspect that his problems are of his own making, am I not still required to show compassion? And what, exactly, would compassionate outreach mean in this situation? Just going into the little chapel to offer a nice homily for the day, so the men could move on through the hall to their pancakes and bacon?

Oh, the Inconvenience!

My attitude would surely have been different if I'd come across some searing human disaster—if a car bomb had exploded, for instance, and several torn people were lying before me in pools of blood. Compassion would have flowed from my heart then. Or if children with huge round eyes and bloated bellies were begging me, wouldn't I have found some food for them, used my checkbook without limit to make sure they received loving care? If I'd faced some gripping human need like that, I have no doubt my compassion and mercy would have surged forth. The problem with the man standing before me, though, was that he and his situation were so . . . inconvenient.

Yes, it came down to that. Without formulating the logic in conscious words, my mind quickly computed the moral calculus and concluded, He knows what's right, he's had some privileges along the way and squandered them on drink; he knows better than that, and so he deserves no pity. I'm sorry to have to admit how these things work in me.

But are you so different? When have you been broadsided with someone's "inconvenient" problem? How did you respond?

According to the Bible, the entire law is summed up in a single command that most often applies to just such actions: "Love your neighbor as yourself."

Why are these five simple words the bottom line from our Judeo-Christian God? Could this common, down-to-earth statement truly be the highest expression of the Lord of all?

Yes. Because the Ground of Being himself loves us beings unconditionally, just as we are. And that is the most profound reality we can know.

And be careful how you understand it. It means not that God loves us because he sees our potential—what he could make out of us if we'd only believe and get our act together. Nor does it mean that he loves us only when the lurid mess we've been swimming in all these years was never a direct result of our own willful concocting. He doesn't clean us up to make us lovable. He loves our unlovable selves while they're still messy. And our Jesus never says, "You made your bed, so lie in it." Rather, he pulls us out of our slumber and says, "I'll be here to help you stay awake, brother; just *notice* me, that's all." Here is more from Jesus:

> ✑ Then the King will say to those on his right, "Come, you who are blessed by my Father; take your inheritance, the kingdom prepared for you since the creation of the world. For I was hungry and you gave me something to eat, I was thirsty and you gave me something to drink, I was a stranger and you invited me in, I needed clothes and you clothed me, I was sick and you looked after me, I was in prison and you came to visit me."
>
> Then the righteous will answer him, "Lord, when did we see you hungry and feed you, or thirsty and give you something to drink? When did we see you a stranger and invite you in, or needing clothes and clothe you? When did we see you sick or in prison and go to visit you?"
>
> The King will reply, "I tell you the truth, whatever you did for one of the least of these brothers of mine, you did for me."
>
> —Matthew 25:34–40

It's stunning to realize that *noticing Jesus* means, most of the time, perceiving the inconvenient folks hovering around on the periphery of our supremely important daily activities. To notice *them,* with a compassionate heart and practical help.

The social responsibility that comes packed with adding Jesus is still a tough theme for me and for all the Jesus-adders as a whole. For we must constantly check to see whether our outreach efforts are becoming stilted, too sterile, unheeding of the warm flesh and blood of individual human beings and their inconvenient problems. Perhaps the social implications of our message are so clearly spelled out in the Scriptures because it's relatively easy to issue a good soul-winning invitation. But I can see that inviting people to notice Jesus requires more than preaching, especially when the one standing before me has listened to all the words before—sometimes in regular payment for a nightly bowl of soup and a clean set of sheets.

Adding to the Mix

Suppose a brother or sister is without clothes and daily food. If one of you says to him, "Go, I wish you well; keep warm and well fed," but does nothing about his physical needs, what good is it?

—*James 2:15–16*

Jesus appointed His people to be the salt and the light of the world. Salt and light affect, even change, the environment in which they are placed. When you rub salt into meat or fish, bacterial decay is, if not arrested, at least hindered. And if you switch on the light something happens: the darkness is dispelled.

—*John Stott, British cleric*

God dwells among the lowliest of men. He sits on the dust heap among the prison convicts. He stands with the juvenile delinquents. He is

there with the beggars. He is among the sick, he stands with the unem-
ployed. Therefore let him who would meet God visit the prison cell
before going to the temple. Before he goes to church let him visit the
hospital. Before he reads his Bible let him help the beggar.

　　　　　—Toyohiko Kagawa, a convert to Jesus from Buddhism

For the Week Ahead with Jesus

In a prayerful moment during the week, use your mind's
"peripheral vision" to see who is there around you in your
ordinary routines. That is, imagine walking through your
typical day . . . *who is there?*

Then walk physically through your day tomorrow and
notice that person, the one who usually slides off your radar
screen of recognition. Determine to see, speak, act as appropriate—if only to offer a friendly word confirming that person's human dignity.

"The first time he came to the door, I didn't recognize him."

Tim told the story of the man's dirty Levi's and white stubble, the coffee stains on his torn shirt. "I thought he was homeless. But why here? Eight miles from town? On a gravel road?"

The man had bushy eyebrows and a crooked jaw. He dressed like one of the last true cowboys.

"Hi, Jack," said Tim, and Jack grinned a yellow grin. After that, he never called. He just showed up. And since Tim worked in the house as a writer, there was no escape. Not that Jack wasn't interesting. After all, he had emigrated from Ireland in his teens and rode the Rocky Mountain range as a cowboy. To this day, he plays the fiddle and the tin whistle and writes ballads about the Old West. But he also desperately needs attention. So there is no conversation with Jack. Only

monologues. After he is in the door, everyone becomes a captive audience.

Once, when Tim heard knocking, he was particularly frustrated. All morning his plans had been thrown off. He took his time finishing the paragraph he was writing, and when he looked out the window, Jack was already halfway to his pickup. Tim hesitated, and then he shrank from the window. He thought about going to the door and calling out, but he didn't. Instead, he waited as Jack turned the pickup in the driveway.

As Jack drove away that day, his dog lay in the bed of the truck, staring back at Tim with its one good eye. He had the urge to swear at it, "Come on, I'm not that bad. I have work to do. Would a banker drop everything if Jack showed up at the office? Would a doctor stop treating patients?" Later, though, when Tim opened the door to leave to get his son from child care, he nearly stepped on a loaf of bread. As always, Jack had brought some day-old bread. He got these loaves at a discount from the grocery store.

Tim picked up the bread and held it, a symbol of Jack—old, but oddly generous. And Tim felt unsettled: *He had brought me something, but he had gotten nothing in return.*

Those Crazy Interruptions!

This chapter, in a sense, offers the opposite side of the coin. Yes, we need to pay attention and have compassion; we also need to keep ourselves from becoming holy doormats.

So, how do you typically respond to a person in need? And what is your experience with people who desperately need attention, as Jack did, and have no qualms about trashing your day to get it?

One thing we notice about Jesus the more we observe him and get to know him is that he always expresses the appropriate emotion, always acts in the appropriate way. He can be gentle; he can be rough. He can be compassionate, zealous, fearful, sad, happy, angry, enraged, quiet, or boisterous—all bound up in his perfect fulfillment of God's command to every human being: "Love each other as I have loved you."

My point? I believe there *is* an appropriate time to *act in self-preservation* as the way of love. And there is the time to give up self-preservation and offer ourselves in self-sacrificial time and energy. The trick is to know, to discern what each situation, day by day in our lives, requires of us.

Here's a case in point from the life of Jesus:

   Jesus entered a house and did not want anyone to know it; yet he could not keep his presence secret. In fact, as soon as she heard about him, a woman whose little daughter was possessed by an evil spirit came and fell at his feet. The woman was a Greek, born in Syrian Phoenicia. She begged Jesus to drive the demon out of her daughter.

"First let the children eat all they want," he told her, "for it is not right to take the children's bread and toss it to their dogs."

—Mark 7:24–27

Basically, here Jesus wants to be left alone in the house. He tells this bothersome woman to "bug off" . . . for now.

In light of this, we can come back to Tim and ponder, *Did Tim do the wrong thing in hiding behind the curtains and letting Jack leave?* I cannot judge it. I've been there, and so have you—under siege by a very needy person whose needs may go far deeper, far beyond the cure of any relational salve we might offer in a moment of friendliness.

For his part, Jesus had his priorities set—and they were important to him. He wouldn't let himself get off track, because it would be uncompassionate to do so. After all, the world, the entire universe—past, present, future—depended on his completing his mission perfectly.

But there's another issue beyond just rationally prioritizing our energies. This other issue is more subtle and probably more crucial to the health of our souls. It involves how we answer this question: Am I *waiting* to live my life . . . or am I living it *now*? Actually, I could word it in several ways:

- If I could just get rid of all these interruptions, then I could finally get something done.
- Once I graduate/get married/land that job/buy that house/get that raise/(add your own "once I" here), I'll get started with my life.
- If only I could find a . . . quiet place to work/a spouse/a vacation spot/(add your own "if only" here), I could . . . (add your own "life-starting" statement here).

Do you see how it's a crucial question? All of us who habitually think this way could benefit from the idea that *the interruptions* are *our life.* These things that come our way, each of them, planned and unplanned, are the fodder for responding in the way that Jesus modeled and taught us. There is no use preparing for the perfect time to start living. Your life is happening already. Now.

So we come full circle. Tim feels guilty about deserting Jack. He knows that he is called by Jesus to compassion. Jesus enters with stories of good samaritans who drop everything to help a neighbor, with commands to love and self-sacrifice, and with a story that also shows him clearly setting limits, though with a heart open to melting, open to showing a bit of inconvenient mercy. For the end of the story with this woman goes like this:

> ✄ "Yes, Lord," she replied, "but even the dogs under the table eat the children's crumbs."
>
> Then he told her, "For such a reply, you may go; the demon has left your daughter."
>
> —Mark 7:28–29

Was Jesus just using a good teaching method here? Or demonstrating the power of reverse psychology? Perhaps. I'm also thinking that maybe it is really all about the interruptions. But I will have to let you work it out from here. You see, my doorbell is ringing. If you will excuse me . . .

Adding to the Mix

The average American today suffers no twinge of conscience when he passes the sick man on the road. He knows he has paid the "Good Samaritan" to come along after him and take care of this rather unpleasant social obligation. But . . . [Christ] expects us to take the role of the Good Samaritan, and not delegate our Christian love and compassion and concern in every instance to a paid professional or functionary.

—Between Two Worlds, *by John B. Anderson*

My command is this: Love each other as I have loved you. Greater love has no one than this, that he lay down his life for his friends.

—Jesus, John 15:12–13

For the Week Ahead with Jesus

For one whole day, or more, try keeping a record of your activities, making an entry every fifteen minutes. Be especially alert to interruptions you experience: people or events. Note how you respond to each interruption.

When you take time later to evaluate your record, think, What typical interruptions in my daily life are actually opportunities in disguise for potentially reaching out with a little compassion?

14. When you long for a sense of community . . .

Just Add Jesus

We gathered around David in my living room and put our hands on his head and shoulders. This young man had started our small fellowship group five years ago, and now he was leaving to begin a new era in his career, moving his home miles away to another part of the country.

We wanted to accomplish so much in that simple act of laying on our hands and praying for him: to bless him, to tell him of our love and concern, to send him off in the strength of Jesus, to assure him of our continued prayers. I believe we also wanted to assure ourselves that somehow the bond would not be completely broken, no matter whether we ever saw him again.

I was struck by the fact that we were saying things in our prayers that we had never had the courage to say to David directly. Why is this act of praying together such a conduit for a kind of

fellowship that we rarely experience otherwise? An expression of love came through, more poignantly, directly, and powerfully than before. But why did we reserve those expressions only for a time of parting? Of course, our love for one another had been there constantly, under the surface, but it had been acknowledged and revealed far too seldom.

I am not lamenting a "problem" here. For I realize that we can never program our recognition of the supernatural bonds that always exist among us. We can only rejoice when our true fellowship is graciously revealed as the bright, shining truth that it continually is.

Look at the Lord's Prayer (for You)

Most of us know by heart what is commonly called the Lord's Prayer, the Our Father, which appears in Matthew's book about Jesus. But let's get theologically picky for a moment. This really isn't our Lord's prayer at all; rather, it's *our* prayer, the one he taught *us* to pray. So where is Jesus' own prayer? It comes in another place in the Bible, in the writings of his beloved friend John. In this part of the Bible, we get to sneak up on Jesus in prayer (as it were) and hear what he is sharing from his heart with his father. We hear what Jesus is thinking about his life and mission. And, most wonderfully, we're let in on what he thinks about his disciples and what he requests from his father for us.

Yes, Jesus prays for *us*—his disciples—"those whom you gave me out of the world." I know that Jesus refers to the original disciples here, but this also includes you and me and any others who will believe in the years ahead. So what does Jesus want for you? Here is how the Lord's prayer begins:

> ✎ Father, glorify me in your presence with the glory I had with you before the world began.
>
> I have revealed you to those whom you gave me out of the world. They were yours; you gave them to me and they have obeyed your word. Now they know that everything you have given me comes from you. For I gave them the words you gave me and they accepted them. They knew with certainty that I came from you, and they believed that you sent me. I pray for them. I am not praying for the world, but for those you have given me, for they are yours.

—John 17:5–9

After this recounting before his Father of his ministry and the fact that his followers have received the message from heaven, Jesus asks for certain specific things for them—for *us*. Please take a moment very soon to read these requests in your own Bible. But for now, I'll just list the wonderful things that Jesus asks for you in John 17 . . .

> *That you will be protected by the name of God;*
> *That you may be one with the other believers;*
> *That you may have the full measure of joy in you;*
> *That you will be kept safe from the evil one;*

That you will be sanctified—cleansed, committed, and growing in the Spirit;

That you may be one with the other believers;

That all who believe because of your words and actions will be blessed, as well—and be part of this wonderful oneness;

That you will be so close to Jesus that others will, indeed, believe because of you;

That you may be one with the other believers;

That you and all Jesus-adders may be one in unity;

That you will arrive someday where Jesus is (in heaven);

That you will see Jesus' full glory someday;

That you will experience in your life the same love that the Father has for his Son;

That you will have Jesus dwelling inside you.

Jesus wants a lot of good things for you! Don't read any further for a moment. Just savor the goodness of all that Jesus prays for you. Then notice: He *really* wants us to be one with others who seek to add Jesus to their lives. Over and over, he asks his Father to make sure this happens.

We can't live this life of adding Jesus in isolation; it just doesn't work. We are called to be a community of faith and commitment. We can know Jesus fully and most gloriously only as we know and care for his people. For those who are looking on at us, it is our love for one another that proves just how powerful Jesus is in ordinary life—that he really is alive and active today among us, in our unity and mutual caring.

So, for our purposes in this chapter, the one prayer of Jesus for us that stands out like a shining star in the heavens is that *"we may all be one."* Wouldn't it be wonderful to see this totally fulfilled in our day? I think of all the strife in the world, all the division, even among people of the same religious faith. Suppose those barriers could be broken down? Suppose, in our praying for one another, in all the myriad languages of humanity, we could break through to one another and be honest about ourselves, our loves and hates, our greeds and compassions?

As our small group found on a happy and sad morning long ago, it is in prayer that our hearts are melted. It was true even of Jesus. Praying together, and praying for one another, makes impossible a competitive spirit, a desire to humiliate or defeat.

No, instead we use words of blessing, words of hope for our neighbors and friends—and even our enemies. I leave you with one such prayer from the apostle Paul, one of the disciples whose life was totally transformed by the God-Man from heaven. His prayer, too, is spoken directly for you. So drink in its blessing:

✍ I kneel before the Father, from whom his whole family in heaven and on earth derives its name. I pray that out of his glorious riches he may *strengthen you* with power through his Spirit in your inner being, so that *Christ may dwell in your hearts* through faith. And I pray that you, being rooted and established in love, *may have power,* together with all the saints, *to grasp* how wide and long and high and deep is the love of Christ, *and to know this love* that surpasses knowledge—that you *may be filled* to the measure of all the fullness of God.

Now to him who is able to do immeasurably more than all we ask or imagine, according to his power that is at work within us, to him be glory in the church and in Christ Jesus throughout all generations, for ever and ever! Amen.

—Ephesians 3:14–21 (Italics added)

Adding to the Mix

By prayer, community is created as well as expressed. . . . Together we reach out to God beyond our many individual limitations while offering each other the space for our own most personal search. We may be very different people with different nationalities, colors, histories, characters and aspirations, but God has called all of us away from the darkness of our illusions into the light of his glory. This common call transforms . . . ourselves into each other's brothers.

—Reaching Out, *by Henri Nouwen*

Is any one of you in trouble? He should pray. Is anyone happy? Let him sing songs of praise. Is any one of you sick? He should call the elders of the church to pray over him and anoint him with oil in the name of the Lord. And the prayer offered in faith will make the sick person well; the Lord will raise him up. If he has sinned, he will be forgiven. Therefore confess your sins to each other and pray for each other so that you may be healed. The prayer of a righteous man is powerful and effective.

—James 5:13–16

For the Week Ahead with Jesus

Spend some time this week reading and thinking about the Lord's prayer for you in John 17. Jesus wants a lot of good things for you. Silently let each of his requests for you sink into your heart and mind.

Suggestion: Make a note card for each one of Jesus' prayer requests, and dedicate an entire day to each. As you go through your routines, look at that card and recall this request of Jesus for you. Open your heart to it, and look for ways that he is fulfilling this thing in you, even now. Then, give thanks.

M y friend Diego (who now holds a Ph.D. in biblical studies) recalls being stumped about certain religious questions long ago. It wasn't comfortable for him, he relates. . . .

I still remember Mr. Gene Driver, my Sunday school teacher in Memphis, Tennessee. He had informed our fifth-grade boys' class that we would be witnessing, and he didn't make it optional. We were to corner our quarry, unleash witness, and report back next Sunday.

Who would my target witness be? It boiled down to Sammy Crump, my best friend. The memory is still vivid. He was a safety patrol boy. There he was, standing in the rain with his yellow raincoat on and carrying his red patrol flag in front of Springdale Elementary School. I figured I could get in a one-minute hit-and-run witness before Sammy boldly stepped out into traffic in

the downpour. So I mumbled a few churchly sounding things about how some people thought they were good enough to make it to heaven without Jesus (I think).

Mission accomplished. Pressure off—at least until Sunday's report. (Incidentally, Mr. Driver also told me that if I could eat a hundred carrots in one day, I would completely clear my acne. That project proved to be a failure, too.)

Here's the thing about the incident that I still ponder today: Sammy came back with a more-than-astute-fifth-grader question that I couldn't answer: "What about all those people in China and Africa who have different religions and never even heard of Jesus?" Since those days I've been sensitive to such questions, kind of on the lookout for them. Because in sharing my faith in Jesus, in my adult years, I've come across some real stumpers. People ask, for instance:

"If the Bible was written by humans, how can it be from God?"
"Who's to say what's really right and wrong—unless you just assume the Bible's true?"
"If God is so loving, why did my son die of cancer?"
"You can't actually prove there's a God, can you?"
"Is God really going to send people to hell—even if they never had a chance to hear about Jesus? Even I wouldn't be that unfair!"
(Add your own recollected stumper here.)

I realize I don't have to be Mr. Answer-All in order to share with a friend about what "adding Jesus" has meant to me. But it bothers me to think how I've not had a ready answer at certain times when I felt I truly needed it. After all, we're not just in a subjective sharing game here, pitting our personal experiences against somebody else's. We're also fellow contributors to the arena of rational discourse.

Sooner or later, in sharing what means the most to us, I believe we'll discover that we need sufficient answers that are meaningful to us and that offer good, solid reasons for our view of reality. What steps can we take to get the necessary grounding, so as to feel comfortable in knowing *why* we believe *what* we believe?

What would you suggest?

My Answers

I'll let you search out your own answers to some of the stumpers Diego listed above. But I can't pass up the opportunity to go back to Sammy myself and try to respond to his question from my own standpoint as an adult.

How shall we, who are adding Jesus, view the other religions? In the Bible (Acts 17, if you'd like to read through it for a moment, right now), the apostle Paul encounters a religion in ancient Athens and displays impressive tolerance toward it. On the other hand, he makes it clear that he offers revealed truth that fulfills and supersedes the wisdom these worshippers already have from their speculations and "their own poets." Paul proclaims Jesus as a unique incarnation of God—and the resurrection as proof of his claims.

In light of Paul's approach, we must apparently hold two natural tendencies in tension. We do wish to accept people who are different, respect other cultures, and give a full hearing to others' sincerely held beliefs. And we will, of course, welcome the good and the true that we find in other religions and refuse to caricature them.

But along with this laudable "tendency to toleration," are we required to hold to a complete relativism about religions? I don't think so. On the other hand, who can be thoroughly objective about religion, anyway? We approach the question from our own various presuppositions and faith commitments. So maybe we can learn from others while continuing to affirm, with Paul, the uniqueness of Jesus' incarnation and resurrection. Perhaps a good approach is the one exemplified by two Christian theologians' thinking in this area:

1. Elton Trueblood's concept of Christianity as "universal preparatory revelation." That is, we recognize two *wrong* ways to approach the question, and one *mediating* way—

Wrong: Since Jesus is the only way, all other ways are completely and totally false in every respect (the fallacy of religious exclusivism);

Wrong: All religions are equally valid, since we are all finite, and each pathway is a possible route to the top of the same mountain (the fallacy of religious indifferentism).

Mediating: Christianity is a fulfillment and development of the truths of the "life of the spirit," many of which can be gleaned within the religions. ("The true light that enlightens every man was coming into the world" [John 1:9].)

2. Richard Niebuhr's concept of "confessing faith." That is, we recognize that our theologies *about* God are finite (having historical limitations); only God is absolute. Thus, we can hold firmly to our beliefs while confessing their incompleteness. This opens us to learning from, and dialoguing with, other worldviews. In this dialogue we find space for genuine, sincere, and gentle witness.

The study of the world religions rarely "weakens" anyone's commitment to Jesus. Rather, it can give us a new appreciation for his uniqueness. The religions come through as philosophies of life, with certain principles being applicable to the *practice* of any faith: such as ego relinquishment (taught by Jesus), love, or pacifism. However, the historical reality of Jesus and his teachings cuts through to a deeper foundation, upon which we build our faith. We, of the Jesus crowd, are not merely ethicists, with effective philosophies of life. We are indwelt, individually and corporately, by the dynamic life of Jesus. And we didn't earn this privilege by our good works; it was given as a free gift.

Two Tough Questions

So, is Jesus really the only way to God? First realize that no one can stand objectively outside the question, claiming to believe in "no religion" until one of them shows itself as more true than the others. We are already practicing faith in some form. That is, everyone has problems and everyone is believing and doing things that they think will solve their problems. On the most foundational level, these beliefs and actions, then, are their "religion." Christianity and the other religions are at hand for your testing as to their ability to solve the big problems like sin (a sense of shortcoming or guilt), longing for security and unconditional love, desire for immortality.

Consider: If a person is depressed, she has various psychotherapy techniques available to solve her problem. To test a particular therapy's effectiveness, she will have to put her wholehearted commitment behind it. Even if she is only half sure her choice is the right one, she'll still have to put her full commitment into it to see if it will work. Therefore she will put full commitment into something only partially understood and believed in. That is, she has faith.

In similar fashion, we approach religious faith. Why Jesus? One reason is that we'll obviously have to start somewhere in our "test." (We don't begin by teaching our toddlers all about how language works; we teach them our particular language.) But moreover, we can recognize that when people have wholeheartedly committed to Christianity, they have discovered a *uniqueness* about Jesus compared to the gods of other religions—the most unique aspect being a claim of historical resurrection. This is not found in the other religions; the supernatural claims and stories are relegated to the realm of mythological gods and heroes that no one claims as historical (see the exploits of Arjuna and Krishna, for example, in the *Bhagavad Gita;* these have a historical backdrop but are not considered to have actually happened in space–time as we know it). They are usually understood to represent aspects of the human psyche.

And the resurrection is either true or not. In gathering the evidence for it, our "wholeheartedly committed" people also claim a personal experience: the indwelling presence of Jesus, being inspired by Scripture reading, warmed by fellowship, called and influenced by the Spirit. But again, all these claims must be wholeheartedly "checked out" by any individual seeker wanting to know the truth.

The worst possible answer to the question, and the most illogical, is to say that because many different claims to truth exist, I will therefore view all of them as relative and equally invalid. We do not approach other everyday claims that way (for example, the claims that different car manufacturers make about their products). Rather, we take the time and energy to check out the claims—and we eventually decide.

Finally, another tough question is, Can I respect another person's beliefs and still help him or her draw closer to Jesus? Of course! But *respect* is the key word. Remember three things:

1. *We are called to witness, but only God can convert.* Do you believe that Jesus has called you and brought you closer to him? If so, you can let him do the calling of others, just as he has called you.

2. *Our witness is both a "confession" of personal knowledge and a recognition of ignorance.* We do not claim to have the whole truth, therefore we can recognize aspects of truth in our friends' beliefs, too. We may believe that reality is a certain way, but we also recognize that it may be different. We could be wrong, and we are willing to have our beliefs put to the test.

3. *No doubt we human beings are in the process of moving either closer or further from the truth of Christ, each moment.* The great Anglican writer and Christian apologist C. S. Lewis put it this way: "The world does not consist of 100 percent Christians and 100 percent non-Christians. There are people who are slowly ceasing to be Christians but who still call themselves by that name. . . . There are people in other religions who are being led by God's secret influence to concentrate on those parts of their religion which are in agreement with Christianity, and who thus belong to Christ without knowing it."

One More Story

Okay, I know this chapter has gotten a little long. But I hope you're sticking with me, because the questions we've been facing are important. Perhaps I've come down a little more firmly on "Jesus-as-the-way" than you would. No problem. And I do want to leave you with one more reminder of the call to tolerance. Remember my friend Lawrence, the missionary? Here he is again . . .

One of my students, a petite Indian woman and devout Hindu, came to me one day and said, "I am giving you this necklace because it is special to our gods. They tell us to wear it and think of them always. Will you wear it and do the same?" It was the end of the semester of an ESL (English as a Second Language) class that I teach at a local college. I received the necklace with gratitude. The student was special to me, and her gesture meant a lot. But what to say? On the spur of the moment, I replied, "Thank you for your gift. Yes, I will wear it. But you must know that my God is Jesus Christ—so I will honor Jesus and pray to Jesus when I wear your necklace. Okay with you?"

She smiled and said, "Of course!"

I struggle every day with this question: How do I accept potential brothers and sisters in Jesus—in their amazing array of lifestyles—and yet be ready to share the uniqueness of Jesus with them? In this instance, I felt happy about the resolution, and yet that very night I began wondering, "Does my student really understand where I'm coming from?"

Besides teaching, I do consultation with corporations seeking to be more effective in other cultures. One executive said to me once, "I used to be into Jesus and all that, but it was just a habit. Now I've thrown it all out, and I'm starting over."

Again, what to say? I'll be perfectly honest. I didn't have a clue. And so, instead of trying to "witness" to this executive, I just tried to be empathetic. I responded, "Do you know something? I believe God would rather you be an honest doubter with deep questions than a phony believer with shallow answers."

He seemed to relax when I said that. And since then, we've had some terrific conversations. We even became close enough so that when I had doubts and questions, he shared with me some things he had learned in his own life.

Maybe after all, people see more of Jesus by what I do than by any pious things I might say. I suspect that executive did. And my Hindu student? During the four months of our class together, I believe she experienced Jesus' love in many subtle ways—in my respect for her as a student, in my personal concern for her family, in my patience every time she interrupted me in class, even as I painstakingly edited the composition she wrote about specific ways she planned to spend a million dollars to renovate the local Hindu temple.

I guess I don't think of converting people. Rather, by the grace of God, I love them. And I feel that they reach out and love me in turn.

Adding to the Mix

I have other sheep that are not of this sheep pen. I must bring them also. They too will listen to my voice, and there shall be one flock and one shepherd.

—*John 10:16*

Faith is a universal human concern. . . . Before we come to think of ourselves as Catholics, Protestants, Jews or Muslims, we are already engaged with issues of faith. . . . We are concerned with how to put our lives together and with what will make life worth living. Moreover, we look for something to love that loves us, something to value that gives us value, something to honor and respect that has the power to sustain our being.

—Stages of Faith, *by James Fowler*

The word religion points to that area of human experience where one way or another we come upon Mystery as a summons to pilgrimage: where we sense beyond and beneath the realities of every day a Reality no less real because it can only be hinted at in myths and rituals; where we glimpse a destination that we can never fully know until we reach it.

—Wishful Thinking, *by Frederick Buechner*

For the Week Ahead with Jesus

During a quiet time this week, think about your ability to offer reasons for your beliefs, in preparation for conversations with someone who might ask, *"Why Jesus?"* Then prayerfully consider how you could improve in this area. Work with these three categories:

- My biggest questions and/or doubts

- Some ways I could pursue "answers" for myself

- A first step I'll take this week

"**B**ecause we're not making sales goals," came the answer, one long and particularly late afternoon. As she walked away from the meeting, Jill really couldn't believe what she'd just heard. She was caught in the middle. Her conscience said this wasn't right, and yet the vice president of her division was ordering her to execute a questionable plan to close out the final month of the fiscal year. The plan was at best on the borderline of being ethical, at worst downright dishonest.

She began to realize that working in a nonprofit, charitable organization can be both a blessing and a curse. And the longer she worked in the corporate headquarters, the more she saw the dark side of things. She came to realize the tremendous ethical dilemma that she'd been drawn into. Her company had a rich heritage of serving the Christian community, yet she began to see

the erosion of the company's reputation as certain corporate decisions began succumbing to selfish motives. And when push came to shove, she could see that it was the customer who got trampled in the process.

The part that troubled Jill the most was the way these business decisions were couched in the language of altruism and goodwill. "This is what is best for the customer" was their mantra, even though they were forcing product into their channels of distribution—things that stores had never ordered.

"I faced many tough questions about myself and about the leadership of the company I worked for," Jill told me. "At times I doubted my abilities and my courage: If I don't do something about this, who will stand up for what is right? Yet I needed this job to take care of my family. If I stood up against the vice president, I would either be fired or labeled a troublemaker. Simply leaving was a tremendous risk that I just couldn't afford to take. But being shuffled off to the management sidelines wasn't a pleasant prospect, either."

Through everything, Jill has wondered about her faith. "My parents always taught me that 'God will provide.' If I really had faith that God would provide, I wouldn't worry about my job or my reputation, would I? I'd stand up for what was ethical and just let the chips fall where they may, right?"

Would Jesus Be Miffed?

What would you do, if you were Jill? And what if Jesus were there, too? How would he react to somewhat dubious business practices? Would he avoid the issue and obey? Would he kindly ask for an interview with his supervisor? Or would he attempt to do his best in his own small area of responsibility and leave the rest to those in authority?

No, none of those.

Here is what I think: he would get white-hot angry. Let's watch him at work for a moment . . .

⚘ When it was almost time for the Jewish Passover, Jesus went up to Jerusalem. In the temple courts he found men selling cattle, sheep and doves, and others sitting at tables exchanging money. So he made a whip out of cords, and drove all from the temple area, both sheep and cattle; he scattered the coins of the money changers and overturned their tables. To those who sold doves he said, "Get these out of here! How dare you turn my Father's house into a market!"

His disciples remembered that it is written: "Zeal for your house will consume me."

—John 2:13–17

Why the anger, whip and all? Isn't this clearly so very unlike our gentle Savior, meek and mild?

One reason many of us may think like that is that the subject of emotions was never talked about by anyone as we were growing up. Perhaps dogma was taught, morality was preached, but no one ever directly discussed or shared about feelings or took an interest in our emotional life.

Oh, we did get edicts regarding emotions, of course—from parents, church, school, and culture:

"Crying only makes things worse."
"Talking back is disrespectful."
"There's nothing to be afraid of."
"Stop your crying or I'll give you something to cry about."
"Christians shouldn't get angry."
"Don't feel bad; with God, you are never alone."
"Lusting after women is sinful, you know."

So, we received negative messages about emotions and no one was there to explain to us the emotional life. Thus we came into adulthood almost totally emotionally repressed. We had honed our intellect and used it to keep our emotions in check. When circumstances occasionally provoke a bubbling of emotions to the surface, we'll be either unaware, embarrassed, or ashamed. And yet . . . *there's that whip in Jesus' hand!* We'll need to understand what was happening here to see what it meant to Jesus and why it produced such a visceral reaction.

First, realize that the Bible tells us that Jesus was fully human and fully divine. While we often point to times when Jesus wept as proof of his human emotions, few of us are as comfortable with the time Jesus expressed anger. When the subject does come up, most quickly point out that Jesus showed righteous anger, to shore up the "fully divine" side of Jesus, and that he did not sin while angry.

But upon taking a closer look at the scene that sparked Jesus' full-on angry response, one can see how *not* feeling anger over the injustice and exploitation is the real sin here.

Yes, Jesus overturned the sales tables of temple-authorized vendors and currency exchange brokers. Animals probably fled from their broken cages, and coin boxes split open when they hit the ground, causing quite a commotion among merchants and worshippers.

He even barred others from bringing their merchandise through the temple courts. Then he spoke to explain his angry actions: "Is it not written: 'My house will be called a house of prayer for all nations'? But you have made it 'a den of robbers'" (Mark 11:17).

Jesus amazed everyone with his teaching. The whole crowd saw that he knew the law, and had responded in righteousness. So how did the chief priests and teachers of the law respond in their moment of accountability? From this moment on, they conspired against Jesus and looked for a way to be rid of him for good.

So what was really going on inside the temple courts that would stir Jesus to anger and the chief priests to plot his murder? After all, the law required each Jewish man to offer live animal sacrifices, and the animal had to pass priestly inspectors to validate the spotless quality of each animal offered. And worshippers routinely traveled far distances, bringing foreign currency to Jerusalem. What better place than right at the temple to set up a currency exchange—or to bring preinspected spotless animals for sale to those who needed them?

The law required that every male Jew pay a temple tax of half a shekel (about two days' pay) every year. But if one came to the temple with foreign currency, he must first exchange his money for the proper Jewish coinage. However this was no simple exchange of coins. And more importantly, the temple condoned and authorized the rate of exchange and policies of the money changers, bringing them conveniently inside the temple courts where they could be easily monitored by the priestly staff.

Now, the exchange of foreign coin for the necessary half shekel would cost you about one-third of the value of the coin being changed. So if you needed change for a dollar, you paid thirty-three cents for the privilege of receiving your dollar back in half shekels. And the bigger the coin offered, the greater the broker's fee and kickback to the chief priests.

While a rich man might grumble over the exorbitant interest charged for changing one coin to another, the practices literally robbed a poor man of his hard-earned wages. Not only this, but other temple-authorized vendors offered preapproved oxen, sheep, and doves for sacrifice at fifty times more than one would pay outside the temple court.

Robbers and thieves indeed—taking from the poor, cheating those who could least afford it—that's what riled Jesus' anger. In public, he courageously stood against blatant social injustice, especially at the hands of the religious leaders, and became marked for death from that moment on. Yes, Jesus was angry. I can only hope to be that angry the next time I witness such an unjust and unrighteous scene.

Now let's allow Jill to finish her story. . . .

After staring at the phone for a whole minute, I pushed my chair back from my desk, took a sip of coffee, and wondered, *Why am I even thinking about this? When I started working in my job nine years ago, I had many dreams, and goals. And yet after numerous project successes, promotions, and increased responsibilities, I'm considering another job that will launch me in a new direction. I know I can stay here in the relative stability and security of a job I've mastered—and perhaps feel guilty about our methods once in a while—or risk a career change and start investing my time and energy elsewhere, where I can also maintain a little more integrity.*

It's certainly difficult to think about leaving; change is scary, and failure is a definite possibility. I've invested nine years in this company, in its products, and in my relationships with coworkers. I've been through both the good times and the bad with this company. And I've stayed because I believe in the company and what it does. But I now feel it powerfully: I'm angry.

As I struggle with the issues, I've come to at least one clear conclusion, though: my work does matter to God. Just knowing that fact, however, doesn't give me the answer to the crucial question facing me right now: Should I pick up this phone and say to the recruiter, "Yes, I'm ready to make a move"? Or should I suck it up and keep hanging in there? (Or pick up a whistle and start blowing?)

Today I, like Jill, face a tough decision. I must choose whether to remain where I am, in relative security and comfort, or to do what I sense an inner calling to do—to launch out on a rather scary new venture. I asked a friend for some advice about the decision. I said, "I feel like I want to hedge my bets." Her response was simply, "Gary, you just can't hedge your bets with Jesus."

I will not forget that word of wisdom. Perhaps real growth in faith only occurs when we put ourselves on the firing line—when following the call means having everything to gain but having something to lose, too. In short, to *have* faith means learning *to live by* faith.

I think of the whole environment of "Christian beginnings"—a time in the history of the world when Jesus' people were called upon to launch a whole new enterprise: the Church. It would have been easier for those first disciples who knew Jesus to bond together, in the comfort and consolation of their fond memories of the Teacher, and live out their days in secluded obscurity. But this was not the plan God had in mind for them. No, they were called to reach out and risk failure, to attempt advancing a kingdom they could barely yet envision.

If the fullest life is a life of faith, then by definition it is a life of risk. I can see that to cease risking, or to run from it, is to die a little bit inside—though it certainly is tempting to run, because risking means being willing to proceed, often in chaotic circumstances, without being sure how things will turn out. As writer Madeleine L'Engle said, "We do not need the sheltering wings when things go smoothly. We are closest to God in the darkness, stumbling along blindly."

Adding to the Mix

Any time you commit to living a more godly life, you are entering enemy territory. Expect spiritual conflict. Whether it is fashionable or not, integrity involves a price, but the cost pales in comparison with the cost of compromise. People can ruin your reputation, but no one can take away your integrity.

—*Paul Kroger, president, Career Impact Ministries*

Women have often lamented that society judges them almost exclusively in terms of their bodies and looks, reducing them to "sex objects." Men are subject to even more impersonal standards; they tend to be judged by their career and salaries, standards which reduce them to "success objects."

—Wingspan: Inside the Men's Movement,
by Christopher Harding

For the Week Ahead with Jesus

Take some time this week to evaluate the career choice you've made (no matter what age you are). During a period of silence, think back to times when you felt highly engaged, energized, refreshed, inspired, or exhilarated by a project that you have done in any of your past jobs. Or this may have taken place in an informal work setting, or for a church committee, for a volunteer organization, or just on your own. Ask yourself:

   ✿   What talents or skills did this project tap into?

   ✿   What are the abilities that I thoroughly enjoyed using in this work?

   ✿   To what extent does my present employment allow me to use these talents, skills, and abilities?

   ✿   What ethical challenges have you encountered in your workplace? How have you dealt with them?

Now spend some time meditating upon Jesus' words in Matthew 6:24:

   ✑ No one can serve two masters. Either he will hate the one and love the other, or he will be devoted to the one and despise the other. You cannot serve both God and Money.

Notice how seriously Jesus takes our attitude toward money and consider the ethical choices you may face in the future related to working for money. Think, Should I re-examine my business and personal dealings to see if they are completely ethical? What hunches do I have about where to begin?

17. When you want to trust others more . . .

Just Add Jesus

"It ain't exactly according to the safety rules, but in the old days this is how we did it all the time." Al spat a wad of tobacco juice after he said those words to me, and I watched the little brown glob travel two stories down to the pavement. We were on a construction job in Orlando, up on a scaffold, trying to finish nailing up the fascia under the roof of a new condo.

Al was a little guy, many years my senior, but wiry and strong, and an excellent carpenter. He stood looking up at a piece of trim whose loose end was far from the edge of our scaffold, impossible for him to reach. So he'd laid a piece of 2" × 12" lumber so that it extended almost 4 feet out over the side of our tiny platform. Then he invited his young apprentice to do the job. "Go on, nail it. I'll be standing right here on the other end."

Though I was a skinny kid at the time, I'm sure I weighed more than Al, and I wanted time to compute the physics of the thing—all the angles and weight tolerances, the board strength and atmospheric conditions—before launching into this experiment in good, old-fashioned ingenuity. To tell the truth, I wasn't so sure I could trust old Al. . . .

Still Competing?

Not even the disciples of Jesus trusted one another very far! Observe:

> Then James and John, the sons of Zebedee, came to him. "Teacher," they said, "we want you to do for us whatever we ask."
>
> "What do you want me to do for you?" he asked.
>
> They replied, "Let one of us sit at your right and the other at your left in your glory."
>
> "You don't know what you are asking," Jesus said. "Can you drink the cup I drink or be baptized with the baptism I am baptized with?"
>
> "We can," they answered. Jesus said to them, "You will drink the cup I drink and be baptized with the baptism I am baptized with, but to sit at my right or left is not for me to grant. These places belong to those for whom they have been prepared."
>
> When the ten heard about this, they became indignant with James and John.
>
> —Mark 10:35–41

Did the others figure that these two hot shots were trying to do an end run around them in the hunt for spiritual
status? That's how I see it. And it still happens today among
folks whose dedication to Jesus seems perfectly solid. But
how do you account for the squabbles (jealousies and power
plays) among those who lived so close to Jesus while he was
on earth?

My simple answer is: I've found over the years that trust
increases *as my need to compete with others decreases.* Have you
found it so?

I've rarely been called to put my life into another person's
hands like I did that day with Al. We were down to the ultimate competition: vying for the choicest spot on the "board-
walk of life or death." But even on the most mundane level,
it is still hard for me to trust another person, or even be his
friend. I think it's our tendency to compete that keeps me
guessing. I'm talking about a very subtle form of competition
here: the need to appear just a little bit wiser, richer, stronger,
or more competent than the next guy.

I did step out on a limb with Al that day so many years
ago—and he didn't let me down. And in my fellowship with
my brothers, I see that I'm called to step out in trust again
and again, mostly in everyday ways, by not revealing confi-
dences; by truly meaning it, and showing it, when I volunteer
to "do whatever I can to help"; by determining to cooperate
for mutual spiritual growth rather than settle for a morsel of
superiority at my friend's expense.

Adding to the Mix

You confide in a fellow guy that you are going through a hard stretch right now, and he says, "I can sure sympathize, Jim. Listen, let's get together soon and do some bonding. Really." And he . . . can't get away from you fast enough. He goes off and talks to other people and he says, "Look out for Jim. He strikes me as unstable. A liability to the team. How can we ease him out of here?"

—The Book of Guys, *by Garrison Keillor*

For the Week Ahead with Jesus

If you competed as a teen in sports or other extracurricular activities, gather pictures and awards from your experiences or look through your school yearbooks. As you contemplate these memories from the past, spend some time journaling your thoughts and feelings along these lines:

- How did competing contribute to my personality today? My self-esteem?

- What was good and bad for me about winning and losing?

- What aspects of competition help me achieve as an adult? What aspects cause me to fear or distrust others?

When I was only ten, my cancer-ridden young father took me with him to the hospital to get his next cobalt radiation treatment. Once inside that antiseptic room, standing next to a huge machine that would shoot cell-killing rays into Dad's swollen abdomen, I watched as he slowly undressed. I didn't know what to do. I needed explanations, warmth, assurance—at the very least some acknowledgment of my bewilderment: "Gary, you are afraid, sad, angry, and rightfully so, for your dad is leaving soon. And that will be tough."

Instead, the male nurse in charge put on a jovial act, cajoling me into being cheerful with him. If only I could have seen my father's face, not just the physical pain he was in, but the pain of my own life at that point, mirrored in his eyes.

Though it's been more than three decades since he died, I
still want to know the man whose picture sits on my shelf, the
young man with thick, wavy hair in the Air Force uniform, the
one who looks a bit like me. Wouldn't knowing more about
him, especially how he related with me so many years ago,
help me know more about myself as a man today? According
to John Bradshaw, author of *Healing the Shame That Binds
You,* the mirroring of emotions is essential to a child's healthy
identity formation. In speaking of the trauma of abandonment, he writes: "Children need mirroring and echoing. These
come from their primary caretaker's eyes. Mirroring means
that someone is there for them and reflects who they really are
at any given moment of time. . . . Abandonment includes the
loss of mirroring [and] remains important all our lives."

Why does all of this remain so important to me even now?
The fact is, all of us want our father's blessing, to be beheld
in the gaze of kind eyes with a look that says, "Child, you are
so precious to me." When Dad is absent at a time when that
validation is so crucial, we will still crave that sense of bless-
edness no matter how old we are. Like the biblical Esau, who
wailed "Bless me—me too, my father!" (Genesis 27:34), the
abandoned child continues to cry out in his lifelong search.

Cries of the Searching Child

Several years ago I was at Florida's Cocoa Beach, enjoying the
surf with my son Tim, when an undercurrent swept up under
us and carried us far from shore. We managed to keep our

faces above the foam, but we were fading fast. Furiously dog-paddling, we made no headway toward land. Finally, I decided to put all my strength into one last drive straight for the shore in hopes of touching bottom. I thought I could talk Tim in and pull him to me from there. As I headed out, I heard the most pitiful cry: "No, Dad, NO! Don't leave me! Please!"

The mournful plea haunted me that night, long after we had safely fallen exhausted on the shore, and for many nights my son's cry has replayed in my mind. It was truly the echo of my own inner voice, only occasionally allowed to have its say over the years, the voice of grief, fear, and abandonment that still resounds in me. For at the age of twelve, I, too, saw my father slipping away from me in the "water," the fluid that filled up his body and finally pulled him under.

So the boy in me still cries out. And that cry takes various forms in any man or woman who has experienced the trauma of paternal abandonment, each plea reflecting the pain of a most foundational loss: *"Dad, please don't leave me!"*

If we're to add Jesus to this scenario, we'll need to find a time in his life when he felt abandoned. So, where else but travel to his cross? There we hear three clear cries ringing out as he faced his own cosmic aloneness (Mark 15:34, Matthew 27:46, Luke 23:46):

"Abba!" (Yes, the Father was really his "daddy.")
"Why have you left me?" (Yes, Jesus really did feel abandoned—but it involved much more for him.)

"Into your hands I commit my spirit." (Yes, eventually even Jesus had to come to a place of acceptance.)

The *first word* of Jesus, "Abba!" is simply a kind of Semitic baby-talk way of expressing closeness; in our language, a baby says "Dada." For me, it brings a powerful sentiment to the surface: *"I'm supposed to have a daddy, too!"*

I remember once lying on my bed with my dad's arm under my head and thinking, *You have such big muscles. You are the strongest man in the world.* That is the way it *should* be. But when it isn't that way, when Daddy is not there to be strong for us, we feel the loss keenly.

Yet it may take years to discover that it is all right to voice the complaint that springs not merely from sadness, but justified anger, too: *"I'm supposed to have a dad, too, just like the other kids! You weren't supposed to be sick, Dad. You weren't supposed to leave. You were supposed to stay and take care of ME!"* That anger, stuffed down, can quickly turn into a depression that surfaces in adult life. That anger's eventual percolation to the surface, though, signals the beginning of grief's healing.

The *second word* of Jesus in the throes of abandonment is just a natural human response: *"Why have you left me?"* In this plea, I find at least four powerful connections coupled with certain sad potentialities in human development:

◆ *"There must be something wrong with me."* (The Potential for Shame) A few years after Dad died, I started feeling lumps in my own body. I was sure I had cancer, just like the kind that had killed my father. I remember riding the high school bus thinking, *If only I can get through this school year, or even the basketball season, then I'll be ready to die.* Such thoughts from a healthy seventeen-year-old kid!

I felt flawed in some way, ashamed of myself for what had happened. I even remember thinking, *Why, God, can't you just let me die, like my dad did?* Surely I should have been able to stop his suffering—or at least die too. In a boy's logic, I had been too strong for Dad. After all, he had collapsed and disappeared just as I was starting to be a rebellious teen. I had been a Little League All-Star pitcher the year before his death. Then, a year later, I couldn't throw a strike to save my life. I became unsure of myself, afraid, nervous—and ashamed of it.

◆ *"I just don't know what to do!"* (The Potential for Confused Decision Making) Losing a father at a young age produces a "guidance gap." The searching son longs for affirmation, but a continuous sense of dissatisfaction with accomplishments takes over. No matter how great, those accomplishments never receive the absent father's approval, raising the false hope that perhaps the next venture will produce the desired approval from . . . somewhere.

In the abandoned son's mind, the endless questions swirl: *What should I do next? Have I been a failure so far? Why do I never feel as though I've done enough? Will I ever come to a place of peace about where I am in life?* One man I know described the guidance gap this way: "I wish I could have just once heard these words from my father before he died: 'Son, I'm so very proud of you.' I think then I could have learned to relax a little in life; sit back and enjoy the ride a little more."

◆ *"I'll never let things get so bad again!"* (The Potential for Controlling Behavior) On the day of the funeral, as we were slowly walking into the church behind the casket, I lagged behind, grappling with a complete sense of bewilderment about how to be. Suddenly, my grandfather gave me the cue: "Get up there and take care of your mother." So . . . the key was to take action? Be responsible? Define the problem, control it, and solve it? This was certainly a manly way of handling the situation. So be it. My dad had been sick, and then he was gone; I myself could at least appear to be strong, reserved, and "in control."

Many men who've had out-of-control pasts begin to believe, "If I can just keep bad things from happening from now on, I'll be okay." The problem manifests itself in how we relate to our families. We end up alienating them as we try to design and control our own futures, make our children turn out just right, build a career path that won't disappoint, and produce a world of satisfaction for ourselves. In the process we lose out on the ways life could gift us with gracious surprises, if we would just loosen our grip a bit.

◆ *"I've got to fill this 'hole in my soul'!"* (The Potential for Addictive Escape) The absent father produces a gaping, yawing "hole in the soul" that won't ever be filled this side of glory. I've come to see, through long experience, that this insatiable chasm can only be made smaller by being inside it and drawing it inward, rather than trying to satisfy it with any number of mood-altering fixes: food, relationships, work, pornography, drugs (the standard favorites). As I allow myself to re-experience my grief when it bubbles up, I can only hope that it will move me to greater awareness of what I *really* want: the unconditional love and acceptance that flows only from God.

The *third word* of Jesus, "Into your hands I commit my spirit," speaks of the movement toward acceptance—and even an ability to gain from the experience of loss. Even though it's true that the absence of a father is a wound a boy or girl carries forever, it does not have to be a deadly wound, grievously sidetracking us on our spiritual journey. Instead, the search can gradually take us up onto the road that leads toward acceptance. Though I will always experience a deep, yearning sadness casting its shadow down through the paths of my days, I also know there is a place of rest in the midst of this search for final acceptance.

Psychiatrist Gerald May, in his book *The Awakened Heart: Opening Yourself to the Love You Need,* speaks of a painful, yet hopeful paradox: It may well be possible to fall in love with a longing that cannot be fully consoled this side of heaven. He writes that we can begin to "feel affection for our longing, to value our yearning, treasure our wanting, embrace our incompleteness, be overwhelmed by the beauty of our need." If such acceptance is possible and is the final stage of grieving (as many have taught), what, exactly, do we learn to accept? *For one thing, we can accept loss as a means of spiritual growth.* Really, by what other means can we grow more dependent upon the heavenly Father, except through the gradual chipping away at our own pretence of independence and self-sufficiency?

The Full Circle of Loss

Yes, I believe God uses loss as a way of moving us closer to him. Certainly loss is the story of me and my dad. Most of my memories of him are from the year of his sickness, the year of my slowly losing him in the back bedroom. Eventually, in the prime of his youth, he became an old man to me, shrunk down to 90 pounds from a robust 210. Through all of this it was tough making eye contact with him, for I was, to my great dismay as I admit it now, ashamed of him.

Yet the promise of our Lord is that all of our loss and all of our shame will one day be turned into rejoicing. So it was a momentous epiphany for me that my uncle had recovered old 8-mm films from my grandfather's closets and had put them on videotape almost three decades later.

And the day I walked into my family room, closed the white plastic blinds, sat down, and pushed the tape into the VCR—that was truly a miracle day. For there on the TV screen—in color, too—burst a gloriously sunny slice of history. And in that marvelous scene, on the front lawn of his own father's home, where the brand-new green '54 Nash Rambler sparkled in the driveway, with his own father looking on, a dad took hold of a chubby two-year-old with pure white hair, all decked out in brown short pants and saddle shoes. He laughed and threw the boy up over his head into the air.

And he lifted his eyes up to that little son's face . . . and looked steadily, with a smiling, loving gaze, indeed.

Adding to the Mix

I do not want to die without leaving a record of my belief that suffering can be overcome. For I do believe it. What must one do? One must submit. Do not resist. Take it. Be overwhelmed. Accept it fully. Make it part of life. Everything in life that we really accept undergoes a change.

—Katherine Mansfield, writer

When I mourn I am filled with pain that seems unbearable at first. . . . Sometimes it turns to tears, and sometimes to quiet moments of reflection. It doesn't matter which. The important thing is that I am made vulnerable, receptive—to more pain? Perhaps, but certainly to God's healing love. And Jesus, who knew the human longing for a departed friend, makes the pain bearable and the loss understandable.

—Colleen Townsend Evans, writer

For the Week Ahead with Jesus

In moments of quiet during this week, spend some time thinking through your "Loss History." Feel those losses again, and let their impact speak to you. Silently consider, Is there any sense of worship mingling with my grief? What does this mean to me?

19. When you'd like to reach out with love's message . . .

Just Add Jesus

I was strolling down Chicago's Michigan Avenue on a sunny afternoon, when a clean-cut young man approached and asked, "Sir, when you die, where do you want to go—heaven or hell?"

Now I like engaging in theological conversations, so I had no problem starting to reply with a few intriguing thoughts regarding the afterlife. He immediately interrupted with, "Just answer the question, sir. Heaven or hell, which one?" Again, I attempted to engage in a conversation about it. But he said, "You're just trying to avoid the issue, aren't you? Heaven or hell; heaven or hell is the only choice. So which do you want?"

Since it was the only choice, you can guess my answer. Then he quickly told me that Jesus was the only way to have my choice, and that his group had come all the way from a large church in Indiana to tell me this. He hoped I would

make the right decision, because "Jesus is your only hope, my friend."

I looked around, saw the colorful Sunday school bus parked by the curb, and also saw several other clean-cut young men stopping other pedestrians with the same heaven-or-hell interrogation. In fact, "Heaven or hell?" seemed to ring out on that corner; it was a kind of spiritual mop-up operation, clearing the sidewalk as people chose alternate routes to their destinations. But no one was dropping to his or her knees to receive Christ as Savior.

What's wrong with this picture? I thought. Obviously these young men are attempting to reach out with the message of God's concern for his world. Nothing wrong with that. And, certainly, we are all choosing a more heavenly or hellish future by our ultimate response to that message.

But . . . what's wrong with this picture?

With Jesus, It's All about Gratitude

We've talked about religious tolerance and "witnessing" in this book already (see Chapter 15), and all of those concepts we raised were bouncing around in my mind for the rest of that day.

Then, later that evening, I contemplated another question: What is the key distinguishing characteristic of a person who has opened her heart's door to let Jesus come closer, if not walk right in? What makes these people attractive in the world? Is it the fact that all such folks are nicer and better behaved than all others? (No, I thought, I know some real nice agnostics—and some real ratty believers.) Is it the fact that they have the "answer" and can articulate the ultimate meaning of life with clever, persuasive arguments? (No, for other answers are being clearly articulated too, and are often attractive enough to win many converts—more than the "heaven or hell" approach!)

I came to this conclusion: The distinguishing quality of the Jesus folks is their sense of *indebtedness*. These people know that pure, undeserved grace is at the heart of their lives, that they have no other claim than the privilege of pointing to its Source. For them, everything is a gift.

Perhaps our outreach with the message of Jesus, then, is mostly an exercise in humility. We can only hope that a gratitude-filled life will be unusual enough to move a few onlookers to ask: "What's with *you*?"

I'm sure something like that must have happened often with a man called John the Baptist, one who knew he'd been grasped by Jesus—and not the other way around. He was a man with a message, a totally committed evangelistic "street preacher," striving to win countless converts. I suppose he would buttonhole people sometimes and confront them with heaven or hell. He certainly wasn't bashful. We do know that he constantly spoke to people of their need to repent, to change their ways, and to get baptized for a new lifestyle. But when people began to say that he was awesome, that he was the Messiah himself, John knew the real score:

✑ John replied, "A man can receive only what is given him from heaven. You yourselves can testify that I said, 'I am not the Christ but am sent ahead of him.' The bride belongs to the bridegroom. The friend who attends the bridegroom waits and listens for him, and is full of joy when he hears the bridegroom's voice. That joy is mine, and it is now complete. He must become greater; I must become less."

—John 3:27–30

Not bashful, but clearly humble. He knew he wasn't a self-made man, so he couldn't tell anyone else how to make a life based on his own example. He could only point.

Point to the one coming after him, who was the light of his life.

I like this John. It's written of him that he traveled the countryside living in caves, proclaiming the heavenly kingdom without fear or embarrassment. He dressed in camel skins. He ate honey and bugs. And he basically says, "This great life I have—it's a gift from heaven."

He's actually *thankful* for that plate of locusts?

Yes.

And lest you think this business about grace and gratitude would sound foreign to Jesus' ears, listen to these poignant and rather sobering words of his: "No one can come to me unless the Father who sent me draws him, and I will raise him up at the last day" (John 6:44). In point of fact, even the ability to add Jesus is given to you and me as a gift.

So . . . you wish to tell a friend about your experience with Jesus? It may be best to avoid jumping right to a discussion of the afterlife. Maybe talk a little about *this* life—*your* life, *today.* How is it *right now* with Jesus? What has he seemed to whisper in your ear lately? And how are you answering?

If there is anything good in this way of traveling through your days, living a life with Jesus added, it will surely show in your eyes. Then you'll no doubt be challenged quite enough just answering the constant query, "What's up with *you* these days?"

Adding to the Mix

If you want to interact effectively with me, to influence me—you first need to understand me. And you can't do that with technique alone. If I sense you're using some technique, I sense duplicity, manipulation. I wonder why you're doing it, what your motives are. And I don't feel safe enough to open myself up to you.

—The Seven Habits of Highly Effective People,
by Stephen R. Covey

Would you know who is the greatest saint in the world? It is not he who prays most or fasts most; it is not he who gives most alms, or is more eminent for temperance, chastity, or justice; but it is he who is always thankful to God, who wills everything that God wills, who receives everything as an instance of God's goodness, and has a heart always ready to praise God for it.

—William Law, *eighteenth-century English cleric*

Do not imagine that if you meet a really humble man he will be what most people call "humble" nowadays: he will not be a sort of greasy, smarmy person, who is always telling you that, of course, he is nobody. Probably all you will think about him is that he seemed a cheerful, intelligent chap who took a real interest in what you said to him.

—Mere Christianity, *by C. S. Lewis*

For the Week Ahead with Jesus

An old song calls us to "Count your blessings, name them one by one." Why not take some time this week to do just that? In a few minutes of silence with Jesus, recall his kindnesses toward you over the years. Then respond:

   ❧   Jesus, I would like to thank you for:

   ❧   Jesus, I need to ask you for:

   ❧   Jesus, please help these people I love:

Appendix

This Awesome Jesus

For nineteen hundred years men have made him the object
of intensive study and have presented pictures
and interpretations of him to the world,
but not one of them satisfies everybody.
This very impossibility of capturing him completely
in a word or phrase,
or in the experience or descriptive powers of any individual,
is a tribute to his greatness.
Rich and poor, learned and unlettered, men of all classes
and all races—all have sought to pour him into their own molds,
because they saw in him some excellence,
some beauty and winsomeness not found elsewhere.
Although Jesus Christ is too great
for our small minds,
yet he is available and adequate
for our every need.

—Source Unknown

He Has Awesome Names for Your Encouragement

Light of the World

🌿 When Jesus spoke again to the people, he said, "I am the light of the world. Whoever follows me will never walk in darkness, but will have the light of life."

—John 8:12

The Gate for the Sheep

🌿 Therefore Jesus said again, "I tell you the truth, I am the gate for the sheep. All who ever came before me were thieves and robbers, but the sheep did not listen to them. I am the gate; whoever enters through me will be saved. He will come in and go out, and find pasture. The thief comes only to steal and kill and destroy; I have come that they may have life, and have it to the full."

—John 10:7–10

The Good Shepherd

🌿 I am the good shepherd. The good shepherd lays down his life for the sheep. The hired hand is not the shepherd who owns the sheep. So when he sees the wolf coming, he abandons the sheep and runs away. Then the wolf attacks the flock and scatters it. The man runs away because he is a hired hand and cares nothing for the sheep.

I am the good shepherd; I know my sheep and my sheep know me—just as the Father knows me and I know the Father—and I lay down my life for the sheep. I have other sheep that are not of this sheep pen. I must bring them also. They too will listen to my voice, and there shall be one flock and one shepherd. The reason my Father loves me is that I lay down my life—only to take it up again. No one takes it from me, but I lay it down of my own accord. I have authority to lay it down and authority to take it up again. This command I received from my Father.

—John 10:11–18

The Resurrection and the Life

✍ "Lord," Martha said to Jesus, "if you had been here, my brother would not have died. But I know that even now God will give you whatever you ask."

Jesus said to her, "Your brother will rise again."

Martha answered, "I know he will rise again in the resurrection at the last day."

Jesus said to her, "I am the resurrection and the life. He who believes in me will live, even though he dies; and whoever lives and believes in me will never die. Do you believe this?"

—John 11:21–26

The True Vine

❧ I am the true vine, and my Father is the gardener. He cuts off every branch in me that bears no fruit, while every branch that does bear fruit he prunes so that it will be even more fruitful. You are already clean because of the word I have spoken to you. Remain in me, and I will remain in you. No branch can bear fruit by itself; it must remain in the vine. Neither can you bear fruit unless you remain in me.

I am the vine; you are the branches. If a man remains in me and I in him, he will bear much fruit; apart from me you can do nothing.

—John 15:1–5

The Bread of Life

❧ Then Jesus declared, "I am the bread of life. He who comes to me will never go hungry, and he who believes in me will never be thirsty. But as I told you, you have seen me and still you do not believe. All that the Father gives me will come to me, and whoever comes to me I will never drive away. For I have come down from heaven not to do my will but to do the will of him who sent me. And this is the will of him who sent me, that I shall lose none of all that he has given me, but raise them up at the last day. For my Father's will is that everyone who looks to the Son and believes in him shall have eternal life, and I will raise him up at the last day."

—John 6:35–40

He Has Awesome Power for Your Life

His Power over Nature

That day when evening came, he said to his disciples, "Let us go over to the other side." Leaving the crowd behind, they took him along, just as he was, in the boat. There were also other boats with him. A furious squall came up, and the waves broke over the boat, so that it was nearly swamped. Jesus was in the stern, sleeping on a cushion. The disciples woke him and said to him, "Teacher, don't you care if we drown?"

He got up, rebuked the wind and said to the waves, "Quiet! Be still!" Then the wind died down and it was completely calm.

He said to his disciples, "Why are you so afraid? Do you still have no faith?"

They were terrified and asked each other, "Who is this? Even the wind and the waves obey him!"

—Mark 4:35–41

His Power to Heal You

One day as he was teaching, Pharisees and teachers of the law, who had come from every village of Galilee and from Judea and Jerusalem, were sitting there. And the power of the Lord was present for him to heal the sick. Some men came carrying a paralytic on a mat and tried to take him into the house to lay him before Jesus. When they could not find a way to do this because of the crowd, they went up on the roof and lowered him on his mat through the tiles into the middle of the crowd, right in front of Jesus.

When Jesus saw their faith, he said, "Friend, your sins are forgiven."

The Pharisees and the teachers of the law began thinking to themselves, "Who is this fellow who speaks blasphemy? Who can forgive sins but God alone?"

Jesus knew what they were thinking and asked, "Why are you thinking these things in your hearts? Which is easier: to say, 'Your sins are forgiven,' or to say, 'Get up and walk'? But that you may know that the Son of Man has authority on earth to forgive sins. . . ." He said to the paralyzed man, "I tell you, get up, take your mat and go home." Immediately he stood up in front of them, took what he had been lying on and went home praising God. Everyone was amazed and gave praise to God. They were filled with awe and said, "We have seen remarkable things today."

—Luke 5:17–26

His Power over All Spiritual Opposition

When they came to the other disciples, they saw a large crowd around them and the teachers of the law arguing with them. As soon as all the people saw Jesus, they were overwhelmed with wonder and ran to greet him.

"What are you arguing with them about?" he asked.

A man in the crowd answered, "Teacher, I brought you my son, who is possessed by a spirit that has robbed him of speech.

Whenever it seizes him, it throws him to the ground. He foams at the mouth, gnashes his teeth and becomes rigid. I asked your disciples to drive out the spirit, but they could not."

"O unbelieving generation," Jesus replied, "how long shall I stay with you? How long shall I put up with you? Bring the boy to me."

So they brought him. When the spirit saw Jesus, it immediately threw the boy into a convulsion. He fell to the ground and rolled around, foaming at the mouth.

Jesus asked the boy's father, "How long has he been like this?"

"From childhood," he answered. "It has often thrown him into fire or water to kill him. But if you can do anything, take pity on us and help us."

"'If you can'?" said Jesus. "Everything is possible for him who believes."

Immediately the boy's father exclaimed, "I do believe; help me overcome my unbelief!"

When Jesus saw that a crowd was running to the scene, he rebuked the evil spirit. "You deaf and mute spirit," he said, "I command you, come out of him and never enter him again."

The spirit shrieked, convulsed him violently and came out. The boy looked so much like a corpse that many said, "He's dead." But Jesus took him by the hand and lifted him to his feet, and he stood up.

After Jesus had gone indoors, his disciples asked him privately, "Why couldn't we drive it out?"

He replied, "This kind can come out only by prayer."

—Mark 9:14–29

His Power for Practical Compassion

e⁄ During those days another large crowd gathered. Since they had nothing to eat, Jesus called his disciples to him and said, "I have compassion for these people; they have already been with me three days and have nothing to eat. If I send them home hungry, they will collapse on the way, because some of them have come a long distance."

His disciples answered, "But where in this remote place can anyone get enough bread to feed them?"

"How many loaves do you have?" Jesus asked.

"Seven," they replied.

He told the crowd to sit down on the ground. When he had taken the seven loaves and given thanks, he broke them and gave them to his disciples to set before the people, and they did so. They had a few small fish as well; he gave thanks for them also and told the disciples to distribute them. The people ate and were satisfied. Afterward the disciples picked up seven basketfuls of broken pieces that were left over. About four thousand men were present. And having sent them away, he got into the boat with his disciples and went to the region of Dalmanutha.

—Mark 8:1–10

His Power over Death Itself

e⁄ Soon afterward, Jesus went to a town called Nain, and his disciples and a large crowd went along with him. As he approached the town gate, a dead person was being carried out—the only son of his mother, and she was a widow. And a large crowd from the town was with her. When the Lord saw her, his heart went out to her and he said, "Don't cry."

Then he went up and touched the coffin, and those carrying it stood still. He said, "Young man, I say to you, get up!" The dead man sat up and began to talk, and Jesus gave him back to his mother.

They were all filled with awe and praised God. "A great prophet has appeared among us," they said. "God has come to help his people."

—Luke 7:11–16

His Followers Have Power, Too!

℞ I tell you the truth, anyone who has faith in me will do what I have been doing. He will do even greater things than these, because I am going to the Father.

—John 14:12

℞ He appointed twelve—designating them apostles—that they might be with him and that he might send them out to preach and to have authority to drive out demons.

—Mark 3:14–15

He Brings You Awesome Blessings!

Blessed Through Christ's Sacrifice

❧ For God was pleased to have all his fullness dwell in him, and through him to reconcile to himself all things, whether things on earth or things in heaven, by making peace through his blood, shed on the cross.

—Colossians 1:19–20

❧ And by that will, we have been made holy through the sacrifice of the body of Jesus Christ once for all.

Day after day every priest stands and performs his religious duties; again and again he offers the same sacrifices, which can never take away sins. But when this priest had offered for all time one sacrifice for sins, he sat down at the right hand of God. Since that time he waits for his enemies to be made his footstool, because by one sacrifice he has made perfect forever those who are being made holy.

—Hebrews 10:10–14

. . . Through Redemption from Sin

❧ [Y]ou were bought at a price. Therefore honor God with your body.

—1 Corinthians 6:20

❧ [J]ust as the Son of Man did not come to be served, but to serve, and to give his life as a ransom for many.

—Matthew 20:28

❧ [A]nd are justified freely by his grace through the redemption that came by Christ Jesus. God presented him as a sacrifice of atonement, through faith in his blood. He did this to demonstrate his justice, because in his forbearance he had left the sins committed beforehand unpunished—he did it to demonstrate his justice at the present time, so as to be just and the one who justifies those who have faith in Jesus.

—Romans 3:24–26

❧ It is because of him that you are in Christ Jesus, who has become for us wisdom from God—that is, our righteousness, holiness and redemption.

—1 Corinthians 1:30

. . . Through Adoption into God's Family

❧ [B]ecause those who are led by the Spirit of God are sons of God. For you did not receive a spirit that makes you a slave again to fear, but you received the Spirit of sonship. And by him we cry, "*Abba,* Father." The Spirit himself testifies with our spirit that we are God's children. Now if we are children, then we are heirs—heirs of God and co-heirs with Christ, if indeed we share in his sufferings in order that we may also share in his glory.

I consider that our present sufferings are not worth comparing with the glory that will be revealed in us. The creation waits in eager expectation for the sons of God to be revealed. For the creation was subjected to frustration, not by its own choice, but by the will of the one who subjected it, in hope that the creation itself will be liberated from its bondage to decay and brought into the glorious freedom of the children of God.

. . . For those God foreknew he also predestined to be conformed to the likeness of his Son, that he might be the firstborn among many brothers.

—Romans 8:14–21, 29

. . . Through Being Born Again

In reply Jesus declared, "I tell you the truth, no one can see the kingdom of God unless he is born again."

"How can a man be born when he is old?" Nicodemus asked. "Surely he cannot enter a second time into his mother's womb to be born!"

Jesus answered, "I tell you the truth, no one can enter the kingdom of God unless he is born of water and the Spirit. Flesh gives birth to flesh, but the Spirit gives birth to spirit. You should not be surprised at my saying, 'You must be born again.' The wind blows wherever it pleases. You hear its sound, but you cannot tell where it comes from or where it is going. So it is with everyone born of the Spirit."

—John 3:3–8

... Through Forgiveness of Your Sins

🖋 Therefore, the kingdom of heaven is like a king who wanted to settle accounts with his servants. As he began the settlement, a man who owed him ten thousand talents was brought to him. Since he was not able to pay, the master ordered that he and his wife and his children and all that he had be sold to repay the debt.

The servant fell on his knees before him. "Be patient with me," he begged, "and I will pay back everything." The servant's master took pity on him, canceled the debt and let him go.

—Matthew 18:23–27

🖋 This is my blood of the covenant, which is poured out for many for the forgiveness of sins.

—Matthew 26:28

Remember the Awesome Events of Jesus' Life

His Birth

🖋 In those days Caesar Augustus issued a decree that a census should be taken of the entire Roman world. (This was the first census that took place while Quirinius was governor of Syria.) And everyone went to his own town to register.

So Joseph also went up from the town of Nazareth in Galilee to Judea, to Bethlehem the town of David, because he belonged to the house and line of David. He went there to register with Mary, who was pledged to be married to him and was expecting a child. While they were there, the time came for the baby to be born, and she gave birth to her firstborn, a son. She wrapped him in cloths and placed him in a manger, because there was no room for them in the inn.

And there were shepherds living out in the fields nearby, keeping watch over their flocks at night. An angel of the Lord appeared to them, and the glory of the Lord shone around them, and they were terrified. But the angel said to them, "Do not be afraid. I bring you good news of great joy that will be for all the people. Today in the town of David a Savior has been born to you; he is Christ the Lord. This will be a sign to you: You will find a baby wrapped in cloths and lying in a manger."

Suddenly a great company of the heavenly host appeared with the angel, praising God and saying, "Glory to God in the highest, and on earth peace to men on whom his favor rests."

When the angels had left them and gone into heaven, the shepherds said to one another, "Let's go to Bethlehem and see this thing that has happened, which the Lord has told us about."

So they hurried off and found Mary and Joseph, and the baby, who was lying in the manger. When they had seen him, they spread the word concerning what had been told them about this child, and all who heard it were amazed at what the shepherds said to them. But Mary treasured up all these things and pondered them in her heart. The shepherds returned, glorifying and praising

God for all the things they had heard and seen, which were just as they had been told.

—Luke 2:1–20

His Childhood

Every year his parents went to Jerusalem for the Feast of the Passover. When he was twelve years old, they went up to the Feast, according to the custom. After the Feast was over, while his parents were returning home, the boy Jesus stayed behind in Jerusalem, but they were unaware of it. Thinking he was in their company, they traveled on for a day. Then they began looking for him among their relatives and friends. When they did not find him, they went back to Jerusalem to look for him. After three days they found him in the temple courts, sitting among the teachers, listening to them and asking them questions. Everyone who heard him was amazed at his understanding and his answers. When his parents saw him, they were astonished. His mother said to him, "Son, why have you treated us like this? Your father and I have been anxiously searching for you."

"Why were you searching for me?" he asked. "Didn't you know I had to be in my Father's house?" But they did not understand what he was saying to them.

Then he went down to Nazareth with them and was obedient to them. But his mother treasured all these things in her heart. And Jesus grew in wisdom and stature, and in favor with God and men.

—Luke 2:41–52

His Baptism

❧ The beginning of the gospel about Jesus Christ, the Son of God.

It is written in Isaiah the prophet:

"I will send my messenger ahead of you,
 who will prepare your way"—
"a voice of one calling in the desert,
 'Prepare the way for the Lord,
 make straight paths for him.'"

And so John came, baptizing in the desert region and preaching a baptism of repentance for the forgiveness of sins. The whole Judean countryside and all the people of Jerusalem went out to him. Confessing their sins, they were baptized by him in the Jordan River. John wore clothing made of camel's hair, with a leather belt around his waist, and he ate locusts and wild honey. And this was his message: "After me will come one more powerful than I, the thongs of whose sandals I am not worthy to stoop down and untie. I baptize you with water, but he will baptize you with the Holy Spirit."

At that time Jesus came from Nazareth in Galilee and was baptized by John in the Jordan. As Jesus was coming up out of the water, he saw heaven being torn open and the Spirit descending on him like a dove. And a voice came from heaven: "You are my Son, whom I love; with you I am well pleased."

—Mark 1:1–11

His Temptations

Then Jesus was led by the Spirit into the desert to be tempted by the devil. After fasting forty days and forty nights, he was hungry. The tempter came to him and said, "If you are the Son of God, tell these stones to become bread."

Jesus answered, "It is written: 'Man does not live on bread alone, but on every word that comes from the mouth of God.'"

Then the devil took him to the holy city and had him stand on the highest point of the temple. "If you are the Son of God," he said, "throw yourself down. For it is written:

"'He will command his angels concerning you,

and they will lift you up in their hands,

so that you will not strike your foot against a stone.'"

Jesus answered him, "It is also written: 'Do not put the Lord your God to the test.'"

Again, the devil took him to a very high mountain and showed him all the kingdoms of the world and their splendor. "All this I will give you," he said, "if you will bow down and worship me."

Jesus said to him, "Away from me, Satan! For it is written: 'Worship the Lord your God, and serve him only.'"

Then the devil left him, and angels came and attended him.

—Matthew 4:1–11

His Apostles

🌿 He called his twelve disciples to him and gave them authority to drive out evil spirits and to heal every disease and sickness.

These are the names of the twelve apostles: first, Simon (who is called Peter) and his brother Andrew; James son of Zebedee, and his brother John; Philip and Bartholomew; Thomas and Matthew the tax collector; James son of Alphaeus, and Thaddaeus; Simon the Zealot and Judas Iscariot, who betrayed him.

—Matthew 10:1–4

His Transfiguration

🌿 After six days Jesus took Peter, James and John with him and led them up a high mountain, where they were all alone. There he was transfigured before them. His clothes became dazzling white, whiter than anyone in the world could bleach them. And there appeared before them Elijah and Moses, who were talking with Jesus.

Peter said to Jesus, "Rabbi, it is good for us to be here. Let us put up three shelters—one for you, one for Moses and one for Elijah." (He did not know what to say, they were so frightened.)

Then a cloud appeared and enveloped them, and a voice came from the cloud: "This is my Son, whom I love. Listen to him!"

Suddenly, when they looked around, they no longer saw anyone with them except Jesus.

As they were coming down the mountain, Jesus gave them orders not to tell anyone what they had seen until the Son of Man had risen from the dead. They kept the matter to themselves, discussing what "rising from the dead" meant.

And they asked him, "Why do the teachers of the law say that Elijah must come first?"

Jesus replied, "To be sure, Elijah does come first, and restores all things. Why then is it written that the Son of Man must suffer much and be rejected? But I tell you, Elijah has come, and they have done to him everything they wished, just as it is written about him."

—Mark 9:2–13

His Triumphal Entry

꩜ The next day the great crowd that had come for the Feast heard that Jesus was on his way to Jerusalem. They took palm branches and went out to meet him, shouting,

"Hosanna!"

"Blessed is he who comes in the name of the Lord!"

"Blessed is the King of Israel!" Jesus found a young donkey and sat upon it, as it is written,

"Do not be afraid, O Daughter of Zion; see, your king is coming, seated on a donkey's colt."

At first his disciples did not understand all this. Only after Jesus was glorified did they realize that these things had been written about him and that they had done these things to him.

Now the crowd that was with him when he called Lazarus from the tomb and raised him from the dead continued to spread the word. Many people, because they had heard that he had given this miraculous sign, went out to meet him. So the Pharisees said to one another, "See, this is getting us nowhere. Look how the whole world has gone after him!"

—John 12:12–19

His Last Supper

꙳ On the first day of the Feast of Unleavened Bread, when it was customary to sacrifice the Passover lamb, Jesus' disciples asked him, "Where do you want us to go and make preparations for you to eat the Passover?"

So he sent two of his disciples, telling them, "Go into the city, and a man carrying a jar of water will meet you. Follow him. Say to the owner of the house he enters, 'The Teacher asks: Where is my guest room, where I may eat the Passover with my disciples?' He will show you a large upper room, furnished and ready. Make preparations for us there."

The disciples left, went into the city and found things just as Jesus had told them. So they prepared the Passover.

When evening came, Jesus arrived with the Twelve. While they were reclining at the table eating, he said, "I tell you the truth, one of you will betray me—one who is eating with me."

They were saddened, and one by one they said to him, "Surely not I?"

"It is one of the Twelve," he replied, "one who dips bread into the bowl with me. The Son of Man will go just as it is written about him. But woe to that man who betrays the Son of Man! It would be better for him if he had not been born."

While they were eating, Jesus took bread, gave thanks and broke it, and gave it to his disciples, saying, "Take it; this is my body."

Then he took the cup, gave thanks and offered it to them, and they all drank from it.

"This is my blood of the covenant, which is poured out for many," he said to them. "I tell you the truth, I will not drink again of the fruit of the vine until that day when I drink it anew in the kingdom of God."

When they had sung a hymn, they went out to the Mount of Olives.

—Mark 14:12–26

His Prayer

Jesus went out as usual to the Mount of Olives, and his disciples followed him. On reaching the place, he said to them, "Pray that you will not fall into temptation." He withdrew about a stone's throw beyond them, knelt down and prayed, "Father, if you are willing, take this cup from me; yet not my will, but yours be done." An angel from heaven appeared to him and strengthened him. And being in anguish, he prayed more earnestly, and his sweat was like drops of blood falling to the ground.

When he rose from prayer and went back to the disciples, he found them asleep, exhausted from sorrow. "Why are you sleeping?" he asked them. "Get up and pray so that you will not fall into temptation."

—Luke 22:39–46

His Crucifixion

 ✑ A certain man from Cyrene, Simon, the father of Alexander and Rufus, was passing by on his way in from the country, and they forced him to carry the cross. They brought Jesus to the place called Golgotha (which means The Place of the Skull). Then they offered him wine mixed with myrrh, but he did not take it. And they crucified him. Dividing up his clothes, they cast lots to see what each would get.

It was the third hour when they crucified him. The written notice of the charge against him read: THE KING OF THE JEWS. They crucified two robbers with him, one on his right and one on his left. Those who passed by hurled insults at him, shaking their heads and saying, "So! You who are going to destroy the temple and build it in three days, come down from the cross and save yourself!"

In the same way the chief priests and the teachers of the law mocked him among themselves. "He saved others," they said, "but he can't save himself! Let this Christ, this King of Israel, come down now from the cross, that we may see and believe." Those crucified with him also heaped insults on him.

At the sixth hour darkness came over the whole land until the ninth hour. And at the ninth hour Jesus cried out in a loud voice, "*Eloi, Eloi, lama sabachthani?*"—which means, "My God, my God, why have you forsaken me?"

When some of those standing near heard this, they said, "Listen, he's calling Elijah."

One man ran, filled a sponge with wine vinegar, put it on a stick, and offered it to Jesus to drink. "Now leave him alone. Let's see if Elijah comes to take him down," he said.

With a loud cry, Jesus breathed his last.

The curtain of the temple was torn in two from top to bottom. And when the centurion, who stood there in front of Jesus, heard his cry and saw how he died, he said, "Surely this man was the Son of God!"

Some women were watching from a distance. Among them were Mary Magdalene, Mary the mother of James the younger and of Joses, and Salome. In Galilee these women had followed him and cared for his needs. Many other women who had come up with him to Jerusalem were also there.

—Mark 15:21–41

His Resurrection

✑ After the Sabbath, at dawn on the first day of the week, Mary Magdalene and the other Mary went to look at the tomb.

There was a violent earthquake, for an angel of the Lord came down from heaven and, going to the tomb, rolled back the stone and sat on it. His appearance was like lightning, and his clothes were white as snow. The guards were so afraid of him that they shook and became like dead men.

The angel said to the women, "Do not be afraid, for I know that you are looking for Jesus, who was crucified. He is not here; he has risen, just as he said. Come and see the place where he lay. Then go quickly and tell his disciples: 'He has risen from the dead and is going ahead of you into Galilee. There you will see him.' Now I have told you."

So the women hurried away from the tomb, afraid yet filled with joy, and ran to tell his disciples. Suddenly Jesus met them. "Greetings," he said. They came to him, clasped his feet and worshiped him. Then Jesus said to them, "Do not be afraid. Go and tell my brothers to go to Galilee; there they will see me."

—Matthew 28:1–10

His Ascension and Return

✐ Do not let your hearts be troubled. Trust in God; trust also in me. In my Father's house are many rooms; if it were not so, I would have told you. I am going there to prepare a place for you. And if I go and prepare a place for you, I will come back and take you to be with me that you also may be where I am.

—John 14:1–3

Recall the Awesome Things He Taught

🍃 Then Jesus went around teaching from village to village.

—Mark 6:6

About Wisdom and Foolishness

🍃 Therefore everyone who hears these words of mine and puts them into practice is like a wise man who built his house on the rock. The rain came down, the streams rose, and the winds blew and beat against that house; yet it did not fall, because it had its foundation on the rock. But everyone who hears these words of mine and does not put them into practice is like a foolish man who built his house on sand. The rain came down, the streams rose, and the winds blew and beat against that house, and it fell with a great crash.

—Matthew 7:24–27

About Forgiveness

🍃 "Two men owed money to a certain moneylender. One owed him five hundred denarii, and the other fifty. Neither of them had the money to pay him back, so he canceled the debts of both. Now which of them will love him more?"

Simon replied, "I suppose the one who had the bigger debt canceled."

"You have judged correctly," Jesus said.

Then he turned toward the woman and said to Simon, "Do you see this woman? I came into your house. You did not give me any water for my feet, but she wet my feet with her tears and wiped them with her hair. You did not give me a kiss, but this woman, from the time I entered, has not stopped kissing my feet. You did not put oil on my head, but she has poured perfume on my feet. Therefore, I tell you, her many sins have been forgiven—for she loved much. But he who has been forgiven little loves little."

—Luke 7:41–47

About Being Alert

❧ Be dressed ready for service and keep your lamps burning, like men waiting for their master to return from a wedding banquet, so that when he comes and knocks they can immediately open the door for him. It will be good for those servants whose master finds them watching when he comes. I tell you the truth, he will dress himself to serve, will have them recline at the table and will come and wait on them. It will be good for those servants whose master finds them ready, even if he comes in the second or third watch of the night. But understand this: If the owner of the house had known at what hour the thief was coming, he would not have let his house be broken into. You also must be ready, because the Son of Man will come at an hour when you do not expect him.

—Luke 12:35–40

About the Right Priorities

And he told them this parable: "The ground of a certain rich man produced a good crop. He thought to himself, 'What shall I do? I have no place to store my crops.'

"Then he said, 'This is what I'll do. I will tear down my barns and build bigger ones, and there I will store all my grain and my goods. And I'll say to myself, "You have plenty of good things laid up for many years. Take life easy; eat, drink and be merry."'

"But God said to him, 'You fool! This very night your life will be demanded from you. Then who will get what you have prepared for yourself?'

"This is how it will be with anyone who stores up things for himself but is not rich toward God."

—Luke 12:16–21

About Showing Mercy

Therefore, the kingdom of heaven is like a king who wanted to settle accounts with his servants. As he began the settlement, a man who owed him ten thousand talents was brought to him. Since he was not able to pay, the master ordered that he and his wife and his children and all that he had be sold to repay the debt.

The servant fell on his knees before him. "Be patient with me," he begged, "and I will pay back everything." The servant's master took pity on him, canceled the debt and let him go.

But when that servant went out, he found one of his fellow servants who owed him a hundred denarii. He grabbed him and began to choke him. "Pay back what you owe me!" he demanded.

His fellow servant fell to his knees and begged him, "Be patient with me, and I will pay you back."

But he refused. Instead, he went off and had the man thrown into prison until he could pay the debt. When the other servants saw what had happened, they were greatly distressed and went and told their master everything that had happened.

Then the master called the servant in. "You wicked servant," he said, "I canceled all that debt of yours because you begged me to. Shouldn't you have had mercy on your fellow servant just as I had on you?" In anger his master turned him over to the jailers to be tortured, until he should pay back all he owed.

This is how my heavenly Father will treat each of you unless you forgive your brother from your heart.

—Matthew 18:23–35

About Persistence

✍ Then he said to them, "Suppose one of you has a friend, and he goes to him at midnight and says, 'Friend, lend me three loaves of bread, because a friend of mine on a journey has come to me, and I have nothing to set before him.'

"Then the one inside answers, 'Don't bother me. The door is already locked, and my children are with me in bed. I can't get up and give you anything.' I tell you, though he will not get up and give him the bread because he is his friend, yet because of the man's boldness he will get up and give him as much as he needs."

—Luke 11:5–8

About Responding to God's Grace

✒ When one of those at the table with him heard this, he said to Jesus, "Blessed is the man who will eat at the feast in the kingdom of God."

Jesus replied: "A certain man was preparing a great banquet and invited many guests. At the time of the banquet he sent his servant to tell those who had been invited, 'Come, for everything is now ready.'

"But they all alike began to make excuses. The first said, 'I have just bought a field, and I must go and see it. Please excuse me.'

"Another said, 'I have just bought five yoke of oxen, and I'm on my way to try them out. Please excuse me.'

"Still another said, 'I just got married, so I can't come.'

"The servant came back and reported this to his master. Then the owner of the house became angry and ordered his servant, 'Go out quickly into the streets and alleys of the town and bring in the poor, the crippled, the blind and the lame.'

"'Sir,' the servant said, 'what you ordered has been done, but there is still room.'

"Then the master told his servant, 'Go out to the roads and country lanes and make them come in, so that my house will be full. I tell you, not one of those men who were invited will get a taste of my banquet.'"

—Luke 14:15–24

About Interpersonal Justice

🌿 Jesus told his disciples: "There was a rich man whose manager was accused of wasting his possessions. So he called him in and asked him, 'What is this I hear about you? Give an account of your management, because you cannot be manager any longer.'

"The manager said to himself, 'What shall I do now? My master is taking away my job. I'm not strong enough to dig, and I'm ashamed to beg—I know what I'll do so that, when I lose my job here, people will welcome me into their houses.'

"So he called in each one of his master's debtors. He asked the first, 'How much do you owe my master?'

"'Eight hundred gallons of olive oil,' he replied.

"The manager told him, 'Take your bill, sit down quickly, and make it four hundred.'

"Then he asked the second, 'And how much do you owe?'

"'A thousand bushels of wheat,' he replied.

"He told him, 'Take your bill and make it eight hundred.'

"The master commended the dishonest manager because he had acted shrewdly. For the people of this world are more shrewd in dealing with their own kind than are the people of the light. I tell you, use worldly wealth to gain friends for yourselves, so that when it is gone, you will be welcomed into eternal dwellings."

—Luke 16:1–9

About Urgently Entreating God

℘ Then Jesus told his disciples a parable to show them that they should always pray and not give up. He said: "In a certain town there was a judge who neither feared God nor cared about men. And there was a widow in that town who kept coming to him with the plea, 'Grant me justice against my adversary.'

"For some time he refused. But finally he said to himself, 'Even though I don't fear God or care about men, yet because this widow keeps bothering me, I will see that she gets justice, so that she won't eventually wear me out with her coming!'"

And the Lord said, "Listen to what the unjust judge says. And will not God bring about justice for his chosen ones, who cry out to him day and night? Will he keep putting them off? I tell you, he will see that they get justice, and quickly. However, when the Son of Man comes, will he find faith on the earth?"

—Luke 18:1–8

About Pride and Humility

℘ To some who were confident of their own righteousness and looked down on everybody else, Jesus told this parable: "Two men went up to the temple to pray, one a Pharisee and the other a tax collector. The Pharisee stood up and prayed about himself: 'God, I thank you that I am not like other men—robbers, evildoers, adulterers—or even like this tax collector. I fast twice a week and give a tenth of all I get.'

"But the tax collector stood at a distance. He would not even look up to heaven, but beat his breast and said, 'God, have mercy on me, a sinner.'

"I tell you that this man, rather than the other, went home justified before God. For everyone who exalts himself will be humbled, and he who humbles himself will be exalted."

—Luke 18:9–14

About Working in the Kingdom

For the kingdom of heaven is like a landowner who went out early in the morning to hire men to work in his vineyard. He agreed to pay them a denarius for the day and sent them into his vineyard.

About the third hour he went out and saw others standing in the marketplace doing nothing. He told them, "You also go and work in my vineyard, and I will pay you whatever is right." So they went.

He went out again about the sixth hour and the ninth hour and did the same thing. About the eleventh hour he went out and found still others standing around. He asked them, "Why have you been standing here all day long doing nothing?"

"Because no one has hired us," they answered.

He said to them, "You also go and work in my vineyard."

When evening came, the owner of the vineyard said to his foreman, "Call the workers and pay them their wages, beginning with the last ones hired and going on to the first."

The workers who were hired about the eleventh hour came and each received a denarius. So when those came who were hired first, they expected to receive more. But each one of them also received a denarius. When they received it, they began to grumble against the landowner. "These men who were hired last worked only one hour," they said, "and you have made them equal to us who have borne the burden of the work and the heat of the day."

But he answered one of them, "Friend, I am not being unfair to you. Didn't you agree to work for a denarius? Take your pay and go. I want to give the man who was hired last the same as I gave you. Don't I have the right to do what I want with my own money? Or are you envious because I am generous?"

So the last will be first, and the first will be last.

—Matthew 20:1–16

Take Hold of His Awesome Promises to You

You'll Have Authority!

❧ Jesus replied, "Blessed are you, Simon son of Jonah, for this was not revealed to you by man, but by my Father in heaven. And I tell you that you are Peter, and on this rock I will build my church, and the gates of Hades will not overcome it. I will give you the keys of the kingdom of heaven; whatever you bind on earth will be bound in heaven, and whatever you loose on earth will be loosed in heaven."

—Matthew 16:17–19

∾ You did not choose me, but I chose you and appointed you to go and bear fruit—fruit that will last. Then the Father will give you whatever you ask in my name.

—John 15:16

You'll Have the Spirit!

∾ And I will ask the Father, and he will give you another Counselor to be with you forever—the Spirit of truth. The world cannot accept him, because it neither sees him nor knows him. But you know him, for he lives with you and will be in you. I will not leave you as orphans; I will come to you. Before long, the world will not see me anymore, but you will see me. Because I live, you also will live. On that day you will realize that I am in my Father, and you are in me, and I am in you.

—John 14:16–20

∾ All this I have spoken while still with you. But the Counselor, the Holy Spirit, whom the Father will send in my name, will teach you all things and will remind you of everything I have said to you.

—John 14:25–26

You'll Have Great Reward!

 And everyone who has left houses or brothers or sisters or father or mother or children or fields for my sake will receive a hundred times as much and will inherit eternal life.

—Matthew 19:29

About the Authors

GARY WILDE, M.Div., a "teacher at heart" and former religious books editor, is a candidate for the Episcopal priesthood. A prolific freelance writer and editor for the major Christian publishers since 1990, he has served as senior copyeditor for Christianity Today's *Leadership Handbooks of Practical Theology* and currently acquires manuscripts for the devotional magazine *Quiet Hour.*

JAMES STUART BELL is the coauthor of *A Cup of Comfort Devotional* and *Christian Miracles,* and the author of the bestselling *Complete Idiot's Guide to the Bible.* He lives in the Chicago area with his wife, Margaret, and has four children.